A Commentary on
EXODUS

A Commentary on
EXODUS

David Pawson

Anchor Recordings

First published in Great Britain in 2019 by
Anchor Recordings Ltd
DPTT, Synegis House, 21 Crockhamwell Road,
Woodley, Reading RG5 3LE

**For more of David Pawson's teaching,
including DVDs and CDs, go to
www.davidpawson.com**

**FOR FREE DOWNLOADS
www.davidpawson.org**

**For further information, email
info@davidpawsonministry.org**

ISBN 978-1-911173-85-4

Printed by Ingram Spark

Contents

This book is based on a series of talks. Originating as it does from the spoken word, its style will be found by many readers to be somewhat different from my usual written style. It is hoped that this will not detract from the substance of the biblical teaching found here.

As always, I ask the reader to compare everything I say or write with what is written in the Bible and, if at any point a conflict is found, always to rely upon the clear teaching of scripture.

David Pawson

READ EXODUS 1–2

The word "exodus" means going out, and it is essentially an escape story. All escape stories are exciting and interesting to read, and the book of Exodus is no exception. I suppose this is the greatest escape in human history. Something of the drama of this story comes through when you realise just what was involved. A military expert has sat down to work out the kind of problems facing this escape. You realise that there were probably over two million people – men, women, and children – to say nothing of thousands of animals. They lived in the most fortified country that the world had then seen. Its borders were held by rows and rows of fortresses. They were so powerful that they had an agreement with every surrounding nation to send fugitives back into Egypt so that it was impossible to escape.

Yet they did – those people got out of chains and escaped from that country. They escaped via the desert, and that in itself is a remarkable story. Here are some of the figures a military general worked out. They would require nine hundred tons of food per day to survive. They would require for cooking 2,400 tons of firewood per day. The very minimum amount of water for survival would be two million gallons per day. If the column travelled in ranks five abreast, the column would be 230 miles long and would take some ten days to walk past. This is to give you some idea of the escape. How on earth did they ever make it? They were led by one man. The very camp where they spent the night would cover five hundred square miles of desert. This gigantic army of slaves escaped from their masters and found freedom.

Now that is the human story, and it would be exciting enough at a human level. But we cannot treat it merely as a human story. If this was purely a human story they would never had made it through that Sinai desert, in which the Egyptian army failed to survive three days in the twentieth century. But the Hebrew people did escape and that event is part of history. Here in the book of Exodus we see God taking a hand in human history. Here we have miracle after miracle. Without those miracles it could not have happened. Those who say there is no God, or those who say that if there is he cannot perform miracles, are absolutely perplexed with the origin of the nation of Israel. They can find no other explanation for their escape from Egypt except a miraculous one. God's greatest acts in the Old Testament are to be found in the book of Exodus. This is the watershed of the history of Israel and to this very day the Jews still celebrate every year the major event of this book in their annual feast of Passover.

But why should Christians read this Exodus? It is part of the Jewish history and it is interesting to them, but why should we read it? Well, it is quite clear that the New Testament is very deeply influenced by the book of Exodus. Word after word from this book comes through into the pages of our New Testament. Words like "covenant", "blood", "lamb", "Passover" and "leaven" come through from the book of Exodus into the New Testament.

There is a greater reason. Why do these words come through? Because the early Christians were Jews? Because the writers of our New Testament were Jews? Because Jesus was born as a Jew and died at the time of the Passover? No, it is because the God of Moses is the God of Jesus. It is the same God in the Old and New Testaments. You are reading about your God. This book tells us wonderful things about our God through what he did for someone else. One of the most encouraging things for a Christian is to hear what God has done for someone else. You say, "He's my God too. He did it for them; he can do it for me."

The fundamental truth that comes out of the book of Exodus is that God is a Redeemer. That means God loves to rescue people from trouble. He loves to get people out of distress. Are you in distress? Are you in trouble? Do you feel the burden of life? Do you feel that things are on top of you? God loves to get you out of that if you will trust him as they trusted him – if you will launch out into the deep as they had to launch out; if you will go out in faith against all odds and put everything in his hands as they did, then you will find that he is the God who redeems.

Exodus follows the book of Genesis and that may sound a rather trite statement, but it is a very important one. There is an order of the books in the Bible. God didn't just jumble them together. The book of Genesis is the history of man's failure to be what God meant him to be. It begins with a beautiful world that is very good. It begins with man being placed in a garden. But the book of Genesis ends with a coffin. This is the story of the tragedy of man's history in a potted version in the book of Genesis. Beginning with every opportunity to love God and to live in a good, unpolluted world, we finish in a coffin. That is the story of our failure. Genesis is the story of man's sin starting with an individual, a woman, spreading to a married couple, Adam and Eve, spreading to their family so that one of their own sons became a murderer and killed another son; spreading to communities, to cities, to societies until God says, "I regret I ever made man," and destroys the whole society. But he begins again with a few more, a man called Noah and his wife and three sons. This little company of people come out of the ark to begin again, into a world that has been washed clean by the flood, and the first thing Noah does is to get drunk and disgrace himself. So it goes on until you finish in Genesis with the people of God, but not in the place where God wants them to be. The reason that you have a coffin mentioned in the last verse of Genesis is that Joseph died in a place where God did not want him to be. They put him in a coffin and, when they left Egypt, in the book of Exodus they brought that coffin and they carried it all the way through, but they were carrying a dead man. He should have been back in the place where God wanted him as a live man.

The reason we have coffins today and the reason that life finishes in a coffin is because even though God created us, we are not in the place where God wants us to be. So Genesis is the story of man's sin finishing in a coffin. Exodus comes straight after, meaning: I am the God who gets you out of this; I am the God who redeems; I am the God who saves; I am the God who rescues; I am the God who says there is an exit. The word "exit" is the same as "exodus". This is why, even from an old book written fourteen hundred years before Christ, a preacher can address you about the God who says today that there is a way out, and God can get people out.

There is a further reason why this is a book for Christians: Jesus was alive before he was born; he was consciously alive as the Son of God from all eternity. Jesus was alive at the time of the Exodus. Jesus was involved in the Exodus. Jesus followed them all the way, and again and again in this book we will see Jesus. We will see the reflection of Jesus in the very events that take place. We see a Passover lamb killed, and the lamb's blood used to protect people from death. We say, "Jesus, the Lamb of God who takes away the sin of the world...." He protects us by his blood.

We shall see in the middle of a desert a rock from which water gushed, and the New Testament says, "The rock that followed them was Christ." We shall see a marvellous building erected in the middle of a desert, a tabernacle for God to dwell in. When we look at the very construction, embroidery and decoration of that building we shall see Jesus. He is involved in all this. For Jesus was just as much alive in the Old Testament as he was in the New, and as he is today. He said, "Search the Old Testament, for it bears witness to me." We shall search this book to learn about Jesus.

Here is one more introductory comment. One day during his earthly lifetime Jesus went up a mountain and had a chat with Moses. They talked together on the top of a mountain. What did they talk about? Luke's Gospel tells us. Though three Gospels describe this event, only one tells us the subject of the conversation. Jesus met Moses—that meant Moses was still alive fourteen hundred years after this book. Moses met Jesus one day, and the unseen world became terribly real to those who were watching. They realised that Moses was still alive and that Jesus knew him.

Luke says, "They spoke together of the Exodus which Jesus was about to accomplish in Jerusalem." Isn't that wonderful? Moses, you brought the Jews out; I'm going to bring the world out; I am going to bring people out. I am going to provide a miraculous way out for all the burdens of people, and I am going to do it in Jerusalem in a few weeks' time. Moses and Jesus had this in common: they both led God's people out.

I have tried to say in my introduction that there are three levels at which you can look at the book of Exodus. First, at the human level, with its human details. It is good to look at it at that level, because the Bible is a very human book. But then we are going to move up to the divine level and ask, "What does this say about God?" Then we are going to move still higher up and say, "This is a Christian book. What does it say to Christians?" Let us look at the first two chapters and look at them three ways. First of all chapter 1: the danger in which the people of Israel had found themselves and got themselves. We look at the human side of the story, and I divide the chapter into three neat little paragraphs, three little parts of the story. Chapter 1 of this first chapter: large families. This is a kind of recap to link with the last few verses of the book of Genesis. Between the book of Genesis and Exodus there is a gap of four hundred years. That is a big gap and things had been happening in that period. Seventy people had come down to Egypt during a time of famine to find food, and therefore had only needed to come down for five years but had stayed there four hundred years. Therein lies a profound lesson. They could have gone back to God's place after five years, but they stayed four hundred.

Just to underline that, the tragedy is there are many people who could come back to Jesus now. They could be back to God today, but they may spend another fifty years away from him. They are doing nothing other than the people of Israel did. It is part of the human story that when you settle in a place you like to stay there. You don't ask, "Does God want me somewhere else?" You think: "I'm happy here," and you settle down. You say, "There's plenty of time to think about a change. Oh, I will maybe start to go to church when I'm in my old age"; or, "Well, some day I will make an attempt and some day I will go and worship," but we settle and we stay.

During that four hundred years there had been phenomenal growth. They had started with a father and twelve sons, and then seventy relatives, and now over two million men, women, and children. Therefore, they became a threat to Egypt. Egypt was very conscious of this growing minority. Wherever you get a minority group of strangers or immigrants in a country and that minority begins to become a very large minority, tension arises between the majority and that minority. In Egypt this minority was now too large and so they decided to burden them with slavery. For 230 years the Jews laboured as slaves. The principle was that if you oppress them, and if you use up their energy in building, and if you work them from dawn to dusk until they are dropping, they are not likely to have so many children. In fact, they found the opposite. They turned shepherds into bricklayers and brick makers, and they used whips on them, but it did not do any good.

So finally, we get to the stage where there was deliberate persecution and even genocide. I want you to notice that Pharaoh was quite happy to let the girls live because he knew that Egyptian men could marry the girls and incorporate them into Egypt. It was the men who were the problem. Pharaoh did not want the men of this strange people to be able to be fathers and fighters.

The midwives were part of the human story. They said, "You know, they are so good at having babies, these Hebrews, they don't need midwives. We always get there too late. It is your Egyptian mothers who take so long to have their babies." It was an amazing reply. Was it true or not? I don't know. God blessed them for it because it was an act of tremendous courage. If it were not true then they would lose their lives as a result. God blessed the midwives and gave them a lovely reward for their loyalty– their own children. Why? Because they feared God more than Pharaoh. That is a wonderful attitude of courage. We fear God more than we fear man, Pharaoh may threaten us but we fear God. If you fear God you don't fear Pharaoh. Now that is the human side of chapter one.

What is there in that for us? Let us look at the divine side of this chapter. What does it say about God? These were God's people – why did he let it happen to them? Why did he allow them to get into slavery, and then into a situation where genocide could be committed? You can ask that question of the crimes of genocide in Nazi Germany and in Britain. For we have been guilty of genocide against the Jews. Anti-Semitism is nothing new. Why does God allow this?

There are two reasons. First of all, his justice: they should not have been there. It is God's justice that chastises. I underline the point that when they first came to Egypt, five years would have seen them through and then they could have gone back to the land of God's blessing. They had come because of famine, and God permitted them to go to get food and be provided for. But they never came back. It was only justice that allowed them to get into trouble. It is justice when a prodigal goes into the far country and finds himself hungry and eating pig's food. It is God's justice but it is something more – it is God's mercy that he allows us to get into trouble when we have wandered out of the place where he blesses. Thank God for the mercy that allows trouble to come. You see, in Egypt they had a rich diet but there were other things there. There were golden calves worshipped in Egypt. Oh, there was plenty of food, but there was plenty of paganism, and plenty of wickedness, and God didn't want them to stay in that sort of place. Through Ezekiel, centuries later, he said to the people of Israel: "Have you still not got rid of your Egyptian habits? Do you not know that I nearly consumed Israel altogether in Egypt?" You find that said in Ezekiel 18. It was as much as to say: I was so cross that you stayed there, I nearly left you there to die. But in his mercy, having allowed them to get into trouble, he said, now I'm going to bring you back.

I have known this, and so have you, and so have many people. Many Christians have known that when you step out of God's will and wander away, and you get content and you stay there, God lets you get into trouble. Thank him that he does. Then he says:now come on out; leave the attractions that have held you there and come back to where I can bless you. That is what chapter 1 says to me about God – that God's justice allowed them to suffer for staying there, but God's mercy said: this will make you want to come back; this will make you want to leave. If they had not been made slaves they would never have wanted to follow Moses into a desert. So God in his mercy lets you suffer that you might want to get back.

There are deeper truths yet for the Christian. Pharaoh is for all time a picture of Satan. Moses (we see in chapter 2) is a picture for Jesus, and Egypt is a picture of sin, as Canaan is a picture of salvation. When I read this chapter and I see Pharaoh I say, "What does that tell me about Satan?" When I read about Egypt I say, "What does that tell me about sin?" You see this Pharaoh did not know Joseph. When you read the life of Joseph you find yourself looking at a life that was so like Jesus. Favourite son of the father, sent to help his brethren, betrayed by the brethren and sold for twenty pieces of silver. Down, down he went until finally he finds himself between two criminals, one of whom he is able to save, and one of whom he is not. From that lowest depth Joseph is lifted up. He is given two titles in Egypt: Saviour and Lord. And when you study the life of Joseph you see Jesus. In Joseph you can see the Saviour.

But here is a king who has arisen who does not know Joseph, who has no relationship with Joseph. In Satan you have someone who has no relationship with Jesus, and Satan does not like to let anybody go to serve God. God says, "Let my people go," and Satan says, "I will not. I'm hanging onto them." And again God says, "Let my people go." If there is one text that is the theme of the book of Exodus it is: let my people go; I want them to be free to serve me. Satan, the Pharaoh of our world, says, "I will not let them go." But God can break the power of Pharaoh and of Satan.

Egypt is a picture of sin. As you know, it is a little fertile land about seven hundred miles long and seven miles wide. It depends on the River Nile, which comes from the melted snows of the hills in Ethiopia and regularly rises and falls each year. It is a low-lying, hot, steaming, stagnant delta. There millions of people can live. There in those days it was a land that was self-indulgent, that had plenty of food, that had lots of rich food—garlic, onions and all sorts of lovely appetising dishes are mentioned in the Bible. The Egyptians were affluent and the land of Goshen was the best land of all. There the people of God found themselves in affluence, in prosperity, with plenty to wear and plenty to eat, and it was so nice they forgot God—this is Egypt.

Sooner or later in every "Egypt" the prosperity gives way to slavery, and the slavery leads to death. Every affluent country that forgets God becomes enslaved and burdened, and leads to a dying society. This is the land of Egypt. One of the texts that is used by the prophet Hosea and later quoted of Jesus, and then applied to God's people, is: "Out of Egypt have I called my son". God says: come out of that kind of situation. Leave it; get back to me. The River Nile, because life was utterly dependent on it, was worshipped as a god. They would bow down, they would throw their children to the crocodiles. They would pray to the River Nile, and this river became the mouth that swallowed up the children of God. When they threw the baby boys in the river they were giving them to their god to destroy. They were asking the Nile god to destroy the people of God. How full of meaning this all is, if you have eyes to see.

We come to chapter two. Again, we look at the human side first. We are first given a picture of Moses among the Egyptians, then among the Hebrews, then among the Midianites—three stages of preparation. From the tribe of Levi, later the priestly family, came this little baby boy. He must have been a lovely baby to look at. In those days a baby was kept in the women's part of the tent or the house for the first three months. Since men were absolutely forbidden to go into the women's quarters, no soldier could enter that part of a house to find out if there was a baby hidden there. The babies were, of course, normally brought out of the house during the day, and shared with the family. But Moses' mother decided to keep this baby boy in the women's quarters for three months hidden. No soldier knew. I can imagine the feverish anxiety when soldiers marched up and down the street, and the mother had to give the baby an extra feed to stop the baby crying. The anxiety would be that he might open his little mouth and exercise his lungs in the time-honoured way. The frightened, fearing mother wondering if he cried whether it would be the death of all of them. This is the drama behind this situation. Then there came a time when she realised she just could not do anything more. She decided on a most bold thing.

She decided to put the baby in the very place where the Egyptian god of the River Nile took babies, and trust her God with that baby. What an amazing thing to do. In the very worst place you might imagine, she said, "I'll just have to let God do something." Making the little papyrus boat, and lining it with tar, she put it in the water, and she left the baby in the place of danger, leaving God alone to look after him and he did. The rest of the story you know so well. It is almost like a romantic fairy tale, isn't it, the princess and the baby?

We see the most ironic thing of all: the baby's own mother being paid to bring him up. This is the amazing way in which God can cause even the wrath of man to praise him, in which God can organise circumstances so that the most unlikely people come to your aid, so that the most remarkable things happen. But this is God manipulating history for his own purpose. God thought this baby needed to be preserved too.

19

He had his eye on the baby.

The child was brought up as a prince. Have you ever been to the Thames Embankment and looked at Cleopatra's Needle, as it is called, the great obelisk with the hieroglyphics on it? Do you know that you are looking at something that Moses saw every day of his life? Do you know that it is one of the two gateposts of the University of Heliopolis? And do you know that through those gates went Moses as a student every day, as Pharaoh's adopted son? Next time you go to London, look at that obelisk and think of Moses, a young man, given the best education at the university in Egypt, looking at that obelisk every day as he walked through. It makes Moses seem just like yesterday. Of course he is still alive, for everyone who puts their trust in God is still alive, but that is where he was brought up.

Then comes this second, rather unfortunate experience. It was the wrong moment for Moses to help his people. It was certainly the wrong method to kill that Egyptian, and it was done in the wrong manner. Moses, at the age of forty, went out to look at the people to whom he belonged. Obviously he had not been near them until then. He had been told that he had been rescued from them. Brought up in the palace, trained in Egyptian manners and customs, now he went out to see the people to whom he really belonged. He saw one of them being ill-treated, and he killed the man who ill-treated him, thinking that nobody saw. He buried the body in the sand and went back to the palace. Pharaoh heard about it, and it was known.

The Hebrews at this stage would not accept Moses as their leader. When he tried to stop the two Hebrews quarrelling the next day they said, "Who made you a prince over us? You are a traitor to our people. You are an Egyptian—you wear their clothes, you live in their palace, you speak their language." They did not realise that God was using all that to prepare Moses to deal with Pharaoh. He ran away.

The third stage is where he meets up with a family and marries one of the daughters. Way down there in the Sinai desert, he wandered around as a shepherd. This prince who knew the best in the fat of the land of Egypt is now a wandering shepherd. But God can do more with a man on his own in a desert than with a prince in all the luxury of the palace. God was really preparing him now. It is a great pity that he married that girl Zipporah. We shall see later in Exodus that because he married outside the people of God, he had rows with her. The first row was over the religious upbringing of his children, and she called him a bloody husband because of what he did. It is a standing warning to men not to marry outside the people of God. It was a mistake. But there he was—he was far from his people, he never thought he would see Egypt again. He thought some little comfort could come to him by getting married and so he did.

He settled down in the desert. He would have stayed there the rest of his life but he was there for another forty years. Here is the life of Moses who lived 120 years: forty years thinking he was somebody—a prince; forty learning he was nobody—far from God, far from his people; and forty years learning what God can do with a nobody, bringing the children of Israel out of Egypt. Well, that is the human side of the story. He married and had a little baby boy. He called him Gershom – stranger, foreigner. He had the first rows with his pagan wife because he wanted the boy circumcised and brought up according to God's people and she did not like it one bit.

Let us look at the divine side, which is so simple. God can order a man's life even before he is a Christian, before he comes to God, to prepare him for what God is going to do. God wanted him in the palace. God wanted him to learn Egyptian. God wanted him to be able to speak to Egyptian leaders, to have the ear of the Pharaoh. So God gave him these great social privileges, but God could not use him in that high social position until God had humbled him and brought him right down. God can only exalt those who have been humbled. God can lift a person to the very top of the social ladder, can give position and terrific responsibility, but can only use them in that position if in private God has brought that person low.

Here then is God's way of dealing with a person. The God who humbles exalts, and you notice that God came and God called when Moses was at the bottom, not at the top. When Moses was sitting alone in the backside of the desert all by himself, feeling that his life had nothing before him, then God revealed to Moses that he was ready to go back to that position for God.

What does this say about the Christian aspect? First, Moses is a picture of the Saviour. There is a little verse at the end of the book of Deuteronomy, the last book that comes from the pen of Moses, where God speaks to Moses, and Moses says to the people of Israel in the name of God these words: the Lord your God will raise up for you a prophet like me from among you. That prophecy Jesus took to himself when he came.

Jesus came to be revealed as a prophet, and much more than that, but a prophet like Moses. Like Moses, Jesus would bring people out of all the selfishness and luxury and sin of their lives, to serve the Lord. When we study the life of Moses we are seeing Jesus. I see Jesus alone in the wilderness, the good Shepherd.

Furthermore, I see in the distance the land of Canaan as the land of salvation, the land of promise, the land of blessing, a land that Jesus wants to bring us to, as Moses wanted to bring the people of Israel. It is not just what you are saved from, it is what you are saved to. It is not just getting out of

Egypt, it is getting into Canaan. It is not just getting out of sin, it is getting into holiness. It is not only getting out of evil, it is getting into good. Moses had this double purpose.

The book of Exodus is not just an escape, it is an elopement. For it is the story of a runaway marriage, the true story of a covenant made between God and his people. God said: "Let my people go that they may come and serve me." It is not just to be saved from Pharaoh, but to be saved to God. This is the story of the book of Exodus – how they began the journey that was to lead to the land of blessing.

The epilogue comes in vv. 23–25. Though they had been very happy in Egypt and got very settled, there came a point where the people of Israel cried. Their cry came up to heaven and God heard. After those four hundred years when they should have been listening to God and praying to him, and they had neglected him, they cried again to God. Did God say, "I'm offended that you've not been listening to me for four hundred years"? Did God say, "I'm not talking to you now"? He didn't talk to them for four hundred years. That is why there is nothing in the Bible between Genesis and Exodus. Did God say, "You've gone too far"? No, God heard and remembered and saw their condition.

He remembered a promise he had made to people who had long since died—Abraham, Isaac and Jacob. He remembered his word. It does not matter how long it has been since God made a promise, he will keep it. You can always claim a promise of God, because he will keep it. God saw, and he did something. In the next chapter we will see what he began to do.

READ EXODUS 3–4

I was standing at the church door and a man came across the road and said, "Why do so many young people come to this church?"

"Because young people of today are looking for reality and they seem to have found it here, but the best way to answer your question would be for you to come and see for yourself," I replied.

"I'm eighty years of age," he responded.

"Well," I said, "I'm going to be talking this morning in church about a man whose life began when he was eighty years of age."

That is our theme. Do you realise that the first two chapters of Exodus cover 480 years? You see, to God time is so different from how it is for us. God picks out what is important to him and you can have a gap of four hundred years and nothing happens of any significance to God. But when he begins to move again, then every day begins to count. A man can live for years and years, and he looks back and feels it has been wasted when he comes to know Jesus. I remember baptising a man aged 72. He had only just become a Christian, and after his baptism he was crying. I said, "Whatever is the matter? You should be joyful and thrilled and pleased."

He replied, "I'm looking back over all the wasted years."

Only what is done in the Lord is of final significance. A man can waste years and so can a nation. The nation of Israel wasted four hundred years and people came and went. These were not the same people who went down into Egypt. They were now perhaps the tenth generation removed. Now here we have Moses and he did not begin his service to the Lord until he was eighty. It took the Lord that long to get him ready—forty years at the top of the social ladder and forty years at the bottom. Forty years living in a palace, in the wealthiest home in the world at that time, and forty years living in a desert in a tent, scratching a living with a few sheep from a bit of scrub bush.

In fact, the Egyptians had a saying that the bottom person in the social ladder is the shepherd. That is quoted in Genesis 46:34 – "Every shepherd is an abomination to the Egyptian." So for forty years he had been given the best food, the best clothes, the best education, the best house, the best company, the best of everything—then he was taken out of all that.

Life began for him at eighty. I hope that remark will act as a brake on young people and an accelerator on the older people reading this. You see, when you become a Christian you are a young, enthusiastic Christian and you want to go off and convert Africa in the first six months. I know, I have been through it, and let me not discourage zeal and enthusiasm. You can start witnessing to the Lord half an hour after you have been converted and you ought to do so. But if you are considering a life's work for the Lord, then the Lord takes time to get you ready for that. You can do damage by rushing off into something that is going to be too big for you.

God the Father kept his own Son Jesus for eighteen years in a carpenter's shop. Have you ever pondered that? He only called him for the last three years of his life to a public ministry of teaching, healing and preaching. Even the great missionary Paul had three years in Arabia before God started his life's work. Albert Schweitzer said he was going to spend his whole life until he was thirty years of age preparing for what God had for him, and then he said, at the age of thirty, "Now Lord, where do you want me to be?"

There is a preparation if you are going to do a big job for God. It is not glamorous, it is not exciting to be alone with God, to be prepared by him, but he can use people who have been through that school. God made Moses mighty in the palace but he made him meek in the desert. Moses was a mighty man but the Bible says he was a meek man as well. From the high position, God had to take him to rock bottom. I have no doubt that at eighty Moses thought his best work was over.

I say to older Christians: don't begin to say that because you are eighty your work for the Lord is over. There are Christians of fifty who start saying, "Oh, we'll give the youngsters a chance. It's time I retired from the Lord's work." It is not. That does not mean you stay in the same office for years, but it does mean that God can take an elderly Christian and start a new work through them.

I think now of a dear old widow—she was very elderly, had white hair, and was always dressed in a black dress, and she lived in a home for the elderly. You know, to her little flat used to come a steady stream of young people. What a ministry she had to the young! They used to come for help, they used to come for advice, and they used to come for comfort. Her life's work in her eighties was marvellous. The Lord can use anybody of any age. He wants all of us in the battle.

Now Moses was alone in the desert, much like Elijah at the brook Kerith, much like Ezekiel sitting at Chebar, much like Paul in Arabia or John on Patmos, or even Jesus in the wilderness before he began his ministry. God got Moses alone. You will never do anything for God in public unless

God can get you alone—that is where it begins. When God gets you by yourself and you are face-to-face with him, and he says, "I want you to do a job and it is between you and me, and I share it with you." Nobody should go into Christian service until they have been alone with God and he has shown them what he is going to do.

Now let us look at what happened at the burning bush. Consider what Moses saw: a bush on fire. That is an unusual thing, though not unknown in the desert. It would be an acacia bush, quite a small, scrubby thing such as you can still see, a very ordinary little bush, but it was ablaze with God. Here, already, at the beginning of Moses' service for the Lord, there is a picture of what his service was to be – a very ordinary bush ablaze with God. God can fill a person with his fire, and far from the fire consuming them, the fire simply fills them. This is what happened on the day of Pentecost when the fire fell and 120 ordinary people had the fire of God on them, and it did not consume them. No, it just drew others to them.

When the fire of God has come upon something or someone, others are drawn. You can still go to a chapel in Wales in the valleys of South Wales and see the chapel where the fire fell. You can still see the very roof where the fire fell, and the village turned out because the chapel was on fire, but there is not a scorch mark on the roof. There was a prayer meeting inside, the fire fell and it did not consume the chapel but it drew the people—they knew that something was happening.

Moses said, "I must turn aside and see this strange sight."

The man who walked over from the bus stop was saying, "I must go and see this strange sight." When every church in this land is on fire, the people will come. They have got to turn aside and see this strange sight. They have been so accustomed to churches like fridges that a church which is warming up is a strange sight. They cross the road and ask why.

Moses, out of nothing more than curiosity, without really thinking about God, just turned aside to see the curious thing. God said, "Moses, Moses." Do you realise that God knows your name before you know his? God knows the name of everybody. That is why sometimes in a congregation somebody says, "Who has been telling the preacher all about me?" They have got the idea that the preacher has been primed by some fond relative or friend to say certain things, I find it is nothing of the kind. God knows every individual before they know him.

"Moses, Moses."

"Who is it?" You can almost see him looking around. It is the God that the great-great-great-grandfather of Moses knew. One wants to say to people who are curious about any church where God is doing things: It's the God your great-great-grandfather knew, but you haven't met him yet; it is so long now since your family went to church that you just don't know him; there is a gap to be bridged. "I am the God of Abraham and Isaac and Jacob." Notice the tense of the verb: God did not say, "I *was* the God of Abraham..." but, "I *am* the God of Abraham..." which means that Abraham is still around and Isaac is still around and Jacob is still around. Believers who have died are still alive because God is their God.

I remember standing in Hebron and looking down at the tombs of Abraham, Isaac and Jacob and their wives. It is one of the really genuine sights of which the archeologists are absolutely sure. There you stand at the tombs of these three and you say, "They are not dead, they are alive. God is their God." God was saying "I am the God of Abraham" long after Abraham had died and been buried in the cave of Machpelah at Hebron.

Can you imagine how Moses felt? He covered his face. God was near. You too could find yourself face-to-face with the living God who is the God of the living. There is no death with God, therefore those who believe in him are the living people. Therefore, he is the God of the living and we do not say that anyone who knows God is dead. They are alive forevermore.

God says "I". Every sentence seems to begin with I – I have heard; I have seen. I am going to do this. I have decided. I promise I will. It is lovely that God says, "I am" and "I will". These are the two great promises: what he is and what he does. The message is: I have seen my people, I know all about them and I am going to bring them out of what they are in, and into something better. When God gets you out of a difficulty he puts you into something better. He not only takes you from something, he takes you into something. He not only gets people from Egypt, he puts them in Canaan— milk and honey flowing.

I remember taking a bus ride down through the Plain of Sharon, and I saw a field in which there were Friesian cows up to their knees in grass. Behind them was a row of beehives. I tried to get a photograph but the bus was going too fast. Flowing with milk and honey – what a place. I'm going to get you out; I'm going to get you in.

Now comes the big surprise: Moses, you are going to do it. That is the crunch; that is the real point of telling him all this. We think of Moses' abortive attempt to help the Hebrews forty years previously. He had probably given up all hope of ever helping them, but now he is told that he is going to do it. Moses is returning to the very place where he had failed, and he is going to succeed. He had wanted to help them; he had tried in his own strength, his own time, his own way. But now, at eighty, he was to do it God's way.

Five times Moses tried to get out of it, and as I read the

next few verses I see myself and you may see yourself. If God says "you go and do this", you can probably think of five hundred reasons why you are not the person to do it. Moses had been too hasty at forty; he was too reluctant to do it at eighty.

Moses' first excuse was that he was an insignificant person. Who am I? He might have done it when he was a prince, but now he felt he was a nobody as a shepherd. People would see his hands and ask: who does he think he is? Just an ordinary working man from the fields. Is this healthy modesty? Gideon said the same thing, Jeremiah said the same thing—you find that many men of God have said this: "Who am I? I'm just an ordinary little person."

It is good to feel inadequate if it drives you to God. It is wrong to feel inadequate if it drives you away from God's work. This is a false modesty—this excessive self-deprecation, which is pride in reverse. There is such a thing as pride in reverse. One sort of pride scrambles for the front seat; another sort of pride in reverse can scramble for the back seat. We can be excessively modest. "Oh, I couldn't do that. I'm not up to that." But God is going to be there and the person he calls has to be there, too. If God calls you to do something, and you say, "Well, I'm a nobody. I'm not the one for this," God may say: I know you're not; that's why I chose you. I'm the one for this, and I'll be with you.

The second excuse is: "I'm ignorant, what shall I say?" If God says "Go and talk to someone", we might reply: "Well, I won't know what to say; I won't be able to answer their questions." Moses asked who he should say sent him. That was because in those days the word "god" was not a name, it was a description. If you had said in those days, "I believe in God," somebody would have said, "Which one?" Nowadays if somebody says, "I believe in God," we have been so brought up on the idea that there is only one that nobody questions which one you are talking about – not in England anyway. But in those days, there were many gods and many lords. Now God gives the most wonderful name. What is God's name? In Hebrew it is *Yahweh*. That comes from the verb "to be," and it is Hebrew for "I am." It tells me three things about God, and when I compare this name with the names of the Egyptian gods, what a difference we find. Yahweh called. "I AM" called.

This means to me, first of all, that God is personal, because only a person says "I am." Secondly, it means he is eternal. It does not matter when you are living, he is always there. It is his eternal name forever. Thirdly, it means that God is unique. You cannot describe him in any other way except by saying he is what he is. He is not like me. He is three-in-one for one thing, and I am not.

To me the most glorious thing about God's name is that it is incomplete. The Hebrews took the word "Yahweh" and made the name bigger for whatever they needed. Here are some of them, "Yahweh Jireh" and that means, "I am your provider; I will provide." Another is "Yahweh Nissi, I am your banner in battle." Another is "Yahweh Shalom", I am peace. Yet another is "Yahweh Tsidkenu", I am your righteousness. Do you need forgiveness? He is your righteousness—what a name.

Moses could listen to all that, and then he could hunt around for another excuse—"They won't believe me." This man is wriggling away from it, isn't he? God makes it clear that the people will believe Moses because of the works that accompany his words. In other words, people will believe the words of God when they see the works of God. The word is confirmed with signs following. If God does not do things when a preacher preaches, then who will believe? God will do things with words that are his, and so he gives Moses three miracles.

The rod of a shepherd is like a cudgel. Of the rod and the staff it is the rod that was used so it is about two feet six long, and used to fight enemies. It is not used on the sheep; the staff is for the sheep. The rod is for the enemies of the sheep – the wild beasts. Yahweh is sending Moses into Egypt with no more weapon than a shepherd's cudgel, but that is enough for all the armies of Egypt. What an amazing thing. "Throw it down on the ground, Moses." God who creates and can create anything in an instant, created a snake. "Pick it by the tail". Of course, it has that lovely little touch that you couldn't see Moses for dust when that happened. He ran away and God said, "Come on back Moses, come back here. Pick it up by the tail," and it was a cudgel again.

"Put your hand inside your cloak," and he took it out and it was white, a leper, unclean. "Put it back in. They will believe you if you do that. Then thirdly, if they still don't, take a bit of water out of the Nile and pour it on the ground. It will turn to blood." Do you realise that every one of these three miracles is a miracle of destruction or threat? For God is not only the God who creates, he is the God who destroys. God can not only give life miraculously; he can give death miraculously. Every one of these three is death. A snake? No wonder Moses ran; it is death. Leprosy – that is death; the water that you drink that produces your food if that turns to blood – that is death. The message here is: show them what my power can do to destroy. You know, people need to realise not only that God can give life but that he can take it away; that he has the power of life and death in his hands. They need to be told not only of heaven where we live forevermore but hell, where people perish. We need to know God's power both ways— and it is a threat.

But Moses, realising that they would believe him, spoke of having a speech impediment. Oh Moses, why don't you just go and do this? We are getting nearer and nearer to the real reason why he wouldn't. What about that speech impediment.? I remember a man who had a speech impediment – a dreadful stammer. It was agony for others when he spoke but he believed that the Lord would help him to pray. I remember hearing him pray and it was beautiful. He still had that impediment when he talked to people, but when he talked to the Lord he sounded just right. That in itself was a greater witness than if the Lord had removed the impediment altogether, because people knew it was the Lord's doing every time he prayed.

Moses said that he was not eloquent, but God can use a person who is not fitted for the job. I knew a retired General who said, "God does not give us the jobs we are fit for; he fits us for the jobs he gives us." That is tremendous, and he has lived by that in his life.

All excuses fall to the ground. We must be sure of only one thing – what the Lord wants us to do. Then we will know we can do it.

Moses jumps to the last thing: "Send someone else." That was the real trouble all along. We have got through to it now. He did not want to go back to where he had been a failure, but God wanted him to.

Moses was told to go back to where he had been a failure, where people knew him, where he had messed things up. Lord, I don't want to. Send someone else. Here am I, send him. He had said, "Here am I" at the beginning but now Moses wants someone else to be sent. God got very cross. Do you realise you can make God cross by trying to push a job onto someone else that he wants *you* to do? God was very angry and sent the brother of Moses to do the talking – you can tell your brother what to say, and he can speak for me. How humiliating for Moses. His brother was going to stand before Pharaoh and he could have done that but he did not want to.

What was really wrong? Moses was questioning two things: God's ability and God's authority—God's ability to use him and God's authority telling him to go. If I produce excuses for not doing something that God wants me to do, it is either because I doubt his ability or I doubt his authority. "Moses, go" – and Moses realised there was no option, that God had called him, and he went.

We look briefly through the last few verses of chapter 4. There are five different reactions to Moses' call. If God calls you to do something, you mustn't expect everybody to shout "Hallelujah!" Some people will not be as thrilled as you are and you may get such different reactions. First of all, his father-in-law approved. He is rather a nice man, this man called Jethro or Reuel (he gets both names here). He comes out as a very wise and very considerate person. It was Jethro who later was going to suggest that Moses had elders to help him with his job. Jethro said, "Yes, you go. Take my blessing with you." It meant, of course, that he was going to say goodbye to his daughter, but happy is the parent who is thrilled when God calls their child to do his work even if it means saying goodbye. Happy is the parent who says, "My blessing is upon you."

It is amazing because he was not a Hebrew. He believed in the religion of the Midianites, which was a very simple religion which was to a degree a true religion in that they believed in one God who made everything that is, and that was their whole creed. That is as far as they got but it was good as far as it went. This dear man Jethro who wasn't a member of the people of God said, "The blessing of the Maker go with you," and that is rather wonderful. He approved and he said, "Peace be with you" – harmony, well-being.

Then there is Pharaoh's reaction; God told Moses before he went: you are going to go right up against Pharaoh; he will be stubborn, he will not want to receive you, he will not let you go, and indeed, I will judge him for this stubbornness by hardening his heart. We will come to the hardening of Pharaoh's heart later. It is a problem at first until you look at it more closely. If you are going to go into the Lord's service, some people may give you their approval and blessing, some unexpected people. Others are going to be antagonistic and will not approve – far from it; they will be against you for doing it.

A third reaction that comes out is in Moses' wife Zipporah. The story behind the next few verses is at best strange, but let us feel our way. Zipporah did not like Moses' religion. He married her before God had called him. She was not sympathetic and she did not like the way the Hebrews carried on in their religion. One of their practices was circumcision, and clearly they had had an argument about it, and Moses had given in to Zipporah, and his sons were not circumcised.

In other words, she was deciding their religious upbringing. On their way to Egypt, they had a row about this, no doubt, and Moses was going to the people of God with uncircumcised sons. He is not really bringing his family with him. Moses fell desperately ill – that is what the Hebrew phrase means when it says "God sought to kill him." Moses talked to his wife Zipporah, and she was so cross that she went off and performed the circumcision. In a disgusting display, she called him names.

From them on, we do not hear of Zipporah until Moses gets back to Jethro in Sinai, and I have the feeling that Zipporah went back home at this point. I am reading between the lines, but she does not appear. It looks as if Moses had to go without her to do his life's work until he came back. It seems like there is a sad situation here, and it may help us to get the human feel of the story. A man called of God and his wife not terribly sympathetic, and indeed, antagonistic and turning back. You can have that when God calls you into Christian service – somebody near and dear to you can be unsympathetic, and that is tough.

The fourth reaction was the reaction of his brother: affection. Aaron set out to meet him. God must have told Aaron to come, and Aaron came and met Moses almost before he had started the journey still within sight of that huge mountain in the Sinai Peninsula, at Mount Horeb. They met and they hugged each other, and Moses told him that they were going to do something together for the Lord. Oh, it was wonderful to have a brother. So after that row with Zipporah, Moses' brother came and gave affection.

Finally, Moses got back to Egypt and the Israelites gathered together, and the people believed. God said they would and they did. So he had the people accepting what God had told him to do. Now this is the kind of pattern that comes when God calls a man or a woman. When God calls you to do something, you will find a variety of human reactions. Some will say, "I'll come with you in this." Some will say, "I don't understand what's got into you. Have you got religious mania?" Some will say, "Well, I don't want you around here." But there will be those who say, "I accept your services from God," and that is the confirmation that God called you.

Now I want you to notice in the last minute the lovely thing the Israelites said. They blessed God because he had already visited them, because he had already decided to rescue them. What faith! The point is this: all the time they had been in their prayer meetings, they had thought that God was up in heaven. They were calling to him, "Lord, get us out of this." Now they realised that God had actually been in the prayer meeting. He had visited them in Egypt and they had not known it. He had been looking round at them. He had seen the way they were treated. Isn't that exciting?

When praying, you are not shouting to a God a long way off. God hears the cry of his people. He visits, he comes, he is there. All the time his people had been crying to God in distant heaven, God had been visiting Egypt – he had been right there and had seen their trouble.

Next time you are praying to God about all your troubles, don't think you have got to tell him all about them. He was there, he saw it all, he knew it all, he visited you.

So they rejoiced. You see, if God has visited your prayer meeting, he is going to do something. If God sees the need, and has decided to act, then you can already bow down and worship. You can already thank him. Do you say "thank you" before you get the answer to your prayer? You only do if you are sure that God has visited you when you prayed. But if you are sure that he did so when you prayed, you say, "Lord, we bow down in worship because you are the living God, and you came and you saw it all."

Why do we worship God? Because he has visited his people. Indeed, through the Holy Spirit, it is not just a visit. He comes to stay.

READ EXODUS 5–10

We are not sure which Pharaoh it was who was speaking at the beginning of Exodus chapter 5. It is one of two and the interesting thing is you can go and look at both the mummified bodies. One of them is that Pharaoh, and inside that body there is a very hard heart.

The nation of Israel, back in 1971, issued a new coin which bore the words in English and in Hebrew: "Let my people go." It was dedicated to millions of Jews in Russia who at that time wanted to escape from the USSR and to get back to the Promised Land.

Yet Israel today is a secular state and many have got back to the Promised Land but have not found their way to the Lord and herein lies the tragedy of God's own people. The reason why God wants to set us free is that we may be bound to him. These are the two sides of the coin. I would like to have seen that Israeli coin come out with two things on it: "Let my people go," on one side in Hebrew and English and then on the other side, "That they may serve me" – and that is the whole point of being redeemed.

"Let my people go" – that is now our theme in this portion of Exodus. The word "redeem" comes in this section and we now know what the word means because of these chapters. It means to let God's people go, to set them free to be God's people, to liberate them from chains, to break their slavery and to let them be free to go and follow God and to do what he wants them to do. Whenever we talk about God redeeming us, whenever we praise our precious Redeemer, that is what we mean; he is the kind of God who breaks chains, sets people free. As the hymn says: "My chains fell off; my heart was free...." What did I do then? I rose, went forth and pleased myself! How contradictory that is and yet sometimes we do just that with the freedom that God has given us. "I rose, went forth, and followed thee" is how it should be. That is the theme of redemption: to be set free to follow, to be set free to worship, to be set free to serve. For by nature none of us is free to serve God; we are too bound up with self-centredness. By nature, we are not free to worship God; we can't see the point of worshipping. We think it is a waste of time and boring. We need to be set free from the kind of self-centred living that is slavery to one's own passions and affections and set free to love God. "Let my people go" – that phrase comes seven times in these chapters. God today looks down on a world in which people are still enslaved in many ways and above all in sin, and the message is: let my people go; I am going to set them free.

There are two phases in the struggle between Moses and Pharaoh. Phase number one was of words; phase number two was of works. In the first phase, God spoke; in the second phase, God acted. In his mercy, God always speaks first; he warns us. He speaks to us; he warns us of what he can do to deal with us, but he gives us the chance to believe his word and to accept it now. He is asking for faith before sight. You see, God has said that those who are guilty of sin are going to hell and many do not believe it. God has said it; Jesus said it; we have got his word for it, but millions don't believe it. They would only believe it if they saw it, but God wants them to believe his word before they see it. For when they see it, then it will be too late, as it was for Pharaoh. The word comes first. God in his mercy, warns us what he will do to those who go on sinning and, in his mercy, he gives us an opportunity to respond first.

Chapters 5–7 cover the phase in which God spoke. Words went backwards and forwards between Moses, God's spokesman through Aaron, and Pharaoh. Moses was caught between three voices. This may be your situation sometime so let me try to describe it. The key word in chapters 5–7 is the little word, "I". Pharaoh said it, Moses said it, and God said it. It all depends in your life which "I" you listen to. The little word "I" comes at you from three directions. It comes to you from those who oppose you. It comes from your own fears and doubts, and it comes from God. Who is the capital "I" in your life? That was the question Moses had to face.

Let us take the first capital "I"—that of Pharaoh. Moses went to Pharaoh and said, "Let my people go." Pharaoh said, "Who is Yahweh that I should take any notice of him?" Let us get the exact words because it is so much "I." "Is that so?" said Pharaoh, "and who is Yahweh that I should listen to him and let Israel go? I do not know Yahweh and I will not let Israel go." Through Pharaoh we can see Satan saying, "I will not let this man go. I will not let this woman go. "I".

Do you know who he thought he was? He thought he was the great I Am; that's who he thought he was. Moses could have given in to the great I Am, who called himself, "Pharaoh". Whenever you seek to liberate people from their slavery and get them redeemed, somebody is going to say, "I will not have this, I will not let them go." That was the first capital "I."

The second "I" arose from the Israelites. Moses was so upset, and you would have been, because the first result of his first visit to Pharaoh was to make the situation ten times worse. A few years ago, an archaeologist was digging in the ruins of Rameses, the city of Egypt referred to here in the book of Exodus. He came across a wall of bricks. It was buried in blown sand from the winds of the Egyptian desert. So he dug away the sand, layer by layer, and the wall was revealed. The top few courses of the bricks were pure clay. The middle third were bricks that were full of bits of wood and rubbish from the dustbins of Egypt. The bottom third of bricks were clay and straw mixed. The archaeologist knew he had discovered the very wall mentioned in Exodus 5.

What was Pharaoh doing when he said, "No more straw?" Well, the simple thing is this: the bricks were made from clay, which was very heavy to dig and to work and slow to dry. The clay was mixed with straw provided by Pharaoh, which made the bricks quicker to dry and lighter to carry. When he stopped the supply of straw, they tried to ease their burden by filling the bricks in with rubbish and scrapping from the desert floor all the bits and pieces they could so that they didn't have to dig so much clay. But when they ran out of rubbish, every brick was solid clay. Imagine the weight and the slowness of drying; they just couldn't keep up with their quota. It was slave labour, sweated labour, and that was the result and they came to Moses. They expressed their feelings that he was messing up the situation and that they were far better off before he had tried to help them.

Now comes the second "I" – that of Moses, who was still trying to get out of it. Three times in these chapters Moses tries to get out of his responsibility. Now he asks: "Why did you ever send me?"

But then comes the third capital "I." God replies to Moses: "I am the Lord and I have made a promise to Abraham, and Isaac, and Jacob" and "I have heard my people" and "I will come and get them out". He is the God of the past, the present, and the future. He had made a promise to Abraham, Isaac, and Jacob. He was going to get his people out. Now here was Moses' dilemma and it is the dilemma that all of us have when God has given us a difficult task to do. There is the big "I" of those who oppose us. There is the "I" within which says, "I am unfit and unable to do it." There is the "I AM" in heaven who says, "I AM the Lord and I have made a promise and I must keep it." Which "I" is going to govern your life? That is the question facing Moses. Is it the "I" of opposition, the "I" of fear or the "I" of Almighty God? That is the issue in chapters 5–7. Praise God, Moses came out of it. He was not going to listen to the 'I' of Pharaoh, nor to the 'I' of Moses. He listened to the "I AM" – God almighty, and because of that, he got his people out. Well it is a very simple little lesson to begin with, but an important one, that wherever you try to do God's work, you are up against a number of different "I am"s, and which one you choose will decide whether you can help people to be free.

Now we move to phase two: from words to works, from God speaking to God acting – doing something, demonstrating his almighty power. There are two phases in God's mighty works. Phase number one was simply a demonstration. Phase number two: destruction – again, God's amazing patience. Martin Luther used to say, "If I were God, I'd have kicked the whole world to bits long ago." But God doesn't do that—we see the patience of God. His message is: look, I will show you what I can do before I do it; I have told you what I will do and you won't listen; I will show you what I will do and see if you listen. Still they wouldn't.

There is something terribly hard about the human heart. Don't ever blame Pharaoh for being such a hard man; you and I have been just like this. Is there anybody who could stand up and say, "I've always paid attention to God's warnings; I've always seen the red light when he's flashed it on? I've always listened to his word and taken it seriously? I've never gone against what I knew to be right"? Every one of us has hardened his heart. We have heard something in church that has gone deep and has spoken to us and by Monday at the latest we have managed to push it out of our minds and hearts and done nothing about it.

Now look at the demonstration of God's power. Just think of it: two old men and a bit of wood, plus God. Moses is eighty years of age, Aaron, eighty-three, and between them there is one lump of wood, used for beating wild beasts off sheep – and they are tackling Pharaoh with the mighty army of Egypt. But you see, two old men and a bit of wood, plus God is a majority; that is all you need. God reveals to them that is all they need to go on to Pharaoh.

At this point, there is an extraordinary thing. We have here the fact that the devil can perform miracles, for when Moses threw his rod down, there were the magicians of Egypt who were dabbling in the occult, and you can perform miracles by the power of Satan. I remember going into the house of a spiritist medium. In that house, every bit of food was being covered with supernatural blood. I opened the pantry door and looked inside, and every plate of food looked as if blood had been tipped on it. The power of Satan was in that house; everything that was taken into it turned to blood. I knew something of the Egyptian magicians turning water into blood. Yes, there are powers that we just don't recognise or realise in the universe today. God has supernatural power, so has Satan. There are miracles of healing done by God and there are miracles of healing done by Satan in our world today. Evil spirits can heal too. Therein lies the danger of seeking healing through a medium.

The power of God was demonstrated by Moses putting the rod down and it turned into a serpent. So did the Egyptian magicians'. Pharaoh said, "My priests can do everything you can do." Then Moses' serpent came and swallowed up theirs; what a picture that is. These are not parallel miracles; one miracle is greater than the other. They were the same miracle to men, but they were not supernaturally because God was behind one miracle and he is more powerful than Satan.

Therefore, God's serpent can swallow Satan's. If ever you find yourself in the position of being attacked by the powers of evil, from supernatural beings, then remember that the supernatural power of God is greater, and his snake can swallow that one. So the demonstration of God's greater power was made. Moses was opposed by Jannes and Jambres, whose names are given to us in the New Testament in 2 Timothy 3, but their power was not enough.

Even though God had demonstrated his power to kill, Pharaoh did not listen and there now began ten dreadful plagues. They were not natural events—I have read school syllabus handbooks that say that these were simply a series of natural events that the people got worried about. Natural events do not start and stop in response to a man's word. Moses said, "I will start it; I will stop it," and he did ten times. Here they are: the water fouled up and became blood, fish died, they had to dig wells to get water to drink. Second: frogs. Now you may not feel that is terribly severe – frogs are rather nice little things. But would you like them crawling in and out of your bedroom? Would you like them all over the place, dying everywhere and stinking? That is what happened—frogs by the million. Three: gnats biting men and animals. Four: flies swarming and ruining the land and covering food and eyes. Five: disease in which the animals began to die—the horses, the camels and the cattle. Six: boils which began to spread from the beasts to the men. Seven: hail so strong it killed every living thing that was outdoors. Eight: locusts. You really have to see a locust plague to believe it; every green thing vanishes. Nine: darkness so dark that nobody could go out. Can you imagine living in a world of perpetual darkness? Ten: the death of the firstborn.

I want you to notice two things about these plagues,

horrible things that they are. First, they get progressively more severe as if God is saying: look, I give you every chance to respond; it is going to be worse and worse; will you please respond? At first it only touched the water. Then it touched the animals; then it touched people, with boils, and then it began to be death. Can you see the progressiveness – a bit of discomfort at first, then disease, then positive danger, and finally death? Still, they did not listen.

Secondly, one of the reasons behind these plagues is this: every single thing of the ten plagues was connected with the pagan religion of Egypt. For example, frogs were part of Egyptian worship. You find them on the old obelisks; you find them carved. Beetles were scarabs. They used to worship the Nile, which was considered by the Egyptians to be a sacred river, like the Ganges and the Nile was the first thing touched. It is as if God is saying: I will touch every part of your religion and I will show that I am in charge of it, not the gods you worship. The result was that Pharaoh's heart was hard. Those are the two phases of these five chapters.

Now let us look at the passage from different people's angles. First, the Hebrew slaves. Do you know that not one of those ten plagues touched them? When the land was in darkness, the sun was shining in that part called Goshen and they had light. When the boils came, their skins were clean and free. When the frogs came, the frogs kept out of their bedrooms. God's people were protected – like a cocoon of love around them. God sent these dreadful things. This proves they were not natural events because if they had been caused naturally, God's people would have suffered with the rest. But when God is going to do something with his people, his protection is around them. From their point of view, can you imagine what they felt like when they saw God's mighty acts of judgment and found that they were safe? It is an amazing experience. I look at Pharaoh's servants. You know, there was a spark of response there. Pharaoh's servants pleaded with Pharaoh: Please, please let them go – can't you see what you are doing? But finally they gave into Pharaoh. Actually, those servants later helped God's people to go; they actually plotted against Pharaoh to set them free.

Let us look into Pharaoh himself. I find him to be a remarkable study. He is a man who on four occasions professes repentance. On four occasions he says, "I'm sorry." On four occasions he says, "Ask God to forgive me." Why then, did Pharaoh never find salvation – when he was sorry and contrite and said he regretted it and was full of remorse? Twice he said "I have sinned" and he asked Moses to pray for him. Yet he was never forgiven. Why? Because his words did not match his heart; he said it, but he did not really believe it. His mind was cunning. All the time, he was working out a way of getting them back again.

He said: "I've sinned; I'll let you go, but worship within the borders of our land." Moses said no. So Pharaoh said, "I've sinned; I'll let you go, but worship near the land, just beyond the border." Moses said no. Then Pharaoh said, "I'm sorry; I'll let you go, but leave your children and wives here." He was thinking: they will come back to their wives. Moses said, "No, we must take them with us."

"Then go, but leave your possessions here; leave your flocks and herds behind." Moses said "No, God wants everything." I could preach a sermon on that, couldn't you?

Satan says, "You can go, but don't go too far into this thing. Don't get religious mania. Don't go right into this Christianity business. Yes, you can go to church once a Sunday, if you like. Come back to me on Monday." We say, in the name of God, "No, God says we must follow him to the Promised Land." "Well then, leave your wives and children; don't be concerned about taking your relatives and friends with you. Have plenty of people still living back in the kingdom of darkness and then that will keep you within reach of me."

"No. I will if I can take my family with me." Every family person must have a deep concern that they should take their relatives with them

"Then leave your possessions behind." You know, possessions are among the ways in which Satan can keep our links with his kingdom.

"I'll look after your property for you, you keep coming back to it."

"No, the Lord wants everything."

He wants me to bring as many people as I can with me, to leave nobody behind if I can help it. He wants me to bring all my possessions because, as Moses said, we do not know which of our possessions God will choose, which he will want, so we must take it all. That is an amazing thought.

Pharaoh was contrite in his speech but cunning in his mind and callous in his heart. Here we come to one of the mysteries of the Bible. At the beginning of these chapters God says, "I will harden Pharaoh's heart." Does that mean that God is simply a chess player, moving people around, hardening this person's heart, softening that? Well, if it were, then quite frankly there would be nothing unfair in that. Paul, writing in Romans 9 says that God has a perfect right to do with anybody what he wishes. After all, he is the potter and we are the clay. Paul writing in Romans 9 mentions Pharaoh and says: if God chooses to harden Pharaoh's heart, that is not unfair. If God chooses a man to demonstrate his power and justice, that is alright and if God chooses another man to demonstrate his mercy that is alright. For what Paul is pleading for in Romans 9 is God's freewill. I believe in freewill; I believe that God has freewill. Some people are so busy talking about human freewill that they allow none to God. I believe in God's freewill. It is God's choice what he does with any of us. If he chooses to harden our heart, that is not unjust. I will tell you why: because we have hardened it first. None of us deserves mercy. If God chooses all of us to demonstrate his punishment, that is only fair. But the ones he chooses to demonstrate his justice are those who have already hardened their hearts.

I notice that in these chapters six times it says "Pharaoh hardened his heart", then four times it says "and God hardened his heart," and it is in that order. Pharaoh hardened his heart six times and so God's message was: "Pharaoh, as a punishment for you, I will harden your heart now. You will not come to me so I can only use you to demonstrate my power, not my mercy. I would have used you to demonstrate my mercy right until now, but now you have gone too far." God had known from the beginning that he would do that, and that Pharaoh would harden his heart. A psalm says: "Today if you shall hear his voice, harden not your heart." If God speaks to you today, if he melts you, if he offers you his mercy, don't harden your heart and say, "I don't need him" or "I don't want to humble myself." Open your heart because there comes a point where you have hardened your heart so much that God says: "From now on, I will harden it. From now on, you demonstrate not my mercy but my justice."

What do these chapters tell me about God? Four things; number one: his power. Do you realise that God has the power to destroy you this minute; that God could wipe me off the face of the earth this minute? Do you realise that that is his power; that it is his power to take away your health, your property, your family? It helps us to worship God reverently if we remember his power.

It also tells me about his will – that God has a right to choose me to demonstrate his love or his anger, to demonstrate his justice or his mercy. He is the potter and I am the clay. It demonstrates his justice. How he punished Pharaoh for hardening his heart. But, above all, it demonstrates his mercy. Why did God give ten plagues? Why did he not just wipe out Egypt and bring his people out in one fell swoop? It is because God is a God of mercy and he wanted to give them every opportunity he could.

There is a parallel between the book of Exodus and the book of Revelation. Six of the ten plagues come back again in the book of Revelation at the end of history: the locusts, the hail, the boils, and death, and others. It says in the book of Revelation that after all the bowls of wrath had been poured out on earth, still men did not repent of their sin. Nothing could be greater proof of the hardness of man's heart than the fact that God has already demonstrated his power in Egypt and in the days of Noah, and still many people do not repent of their sin. But his mercy will rescue his people.

When the mercy of God brought the Hebrews out of slavery, the cost of that was the demonstration of his justice on Pharaoh, and Pharaoh suffered that God's people might be free. The amazing difference between the Old and the New Testaments is this: in the New Testament it was not Pharaoh who suffered, but Jesus.

You cannot set people free without suffering. You cannot set people free from an evil situation without someone paying the cost of that evil. In the New Testament, praise God, it was Jesus. The plagues of sin came on Jesus and the wrath of God came on Jesus. It is only because Jesus on the cross suffered the wrath of God that his people can now be free to worship and to serve. "Let my people go...." Are you free? Has God set you free? It is because Jesus died, and for no other reason.

READ EXODUS 11–12

More years ago than I care to remember, I was playing with a gang of other boys in the street in Newcastle in which I was brought up, and suddenly we came across a patch of blood on the pavement. Of course, little boys can soon imagine all kinds of things having happened so we began to speculate about this blood and then we noticed that it was all over a gate and then on the posts of the gate. Then we saw it was on the front door of the house and then of course we used to have all sorts of rumours among ourselves as to what dreadful deed had been happening.

It was only later when I got home and mentioned this to my parents that they told me that this was a Jewish family and that they did this once a year and that if I looked out next year at the end of March I would see the same thing. They told me why they did it: they were doing something that has been done every year for well over three thousand years. In that house, they had killed a lamb and they had taken its blood which they sprinkled on the gateway and the doorpost as they went in.

To the Jews, Passover is the greatest festival of the year. It goes back to the days when their nation was born, when their calendar was altered. It goes back to the days when God stretched down a mighty hand from heaven and brought them out of slavery and into freedom and made them a free people. Every year they celebrate this Passover. But, you know, the Passover is also a great time for Christians. Here is some of the language that comes in the New Testament. Luke's Gospel says that when Jesus and Moses met on the Mount of Transfiguration, they talked together of the Exodus that he was about to accomplish in the city of Jerusalem. Moses was not the only person who brought people out in a gigantic exodus into freedom; Jesus did the same thing. Furthermore, there is a text in 1 Corinthians 5:7 – "Christ our Passover lamb has been sacrificed for us". Moreover, the language of Exodus 11–13 comes straight through into Christian hymns and into our prayers. Whenever we talk about "sprinkled with the blood" we are going back to the Passover. Whenever we call Jesus the "Lamb of God" we are going back to the Passover. Whenever we say and we mean it that we are washed in the blood, we are going back to the Passover. Whenever we call Jesus the Lamb of God, we are going back to the Passover; we are using Jewish language. Therefore, a study of the Passover will help us to know Jesus Christ.

Exodus 11 begins with Pharaoh's final rejection of God's last word to him. It is a very sad story. Over twelve months God had spoken to Pharaoh again and again. He had now spoken nine times and this man would not listen. This is one of the frustrations and tragedies of life in our world: you can bring a message from God, and people could not care less. You can tell them what their very Creator has said and they remain unmoved and they do not respond.

Why did Pharaoh reject God's word? There are two simple reasons behind this and they lie behind every rejection of God. Number one, he had no faith in God's words; he did not take God seriously. When God said something, he did not believe it. He did not think that God meant what he said. The second thing that led to his rejection is that he had no fear in God's works. He thought that God would not do anything to him. Even though he had demonstration after demonstration of God's almighty power to destroy as well as to save, he never thought that God would touch him.

These two things make a heart very hard. If you do not take seriously what God says and does, your heart gets harder and harder until the point is reached where God himself will write you off. Now I want to apply that very personally today. I find that today I am up against the same two things. First of all, people do not take seriously God's word. I will give you only one example. God, in his word says that sin will be punished by death. Who takes that seriously? Who believes that every act of temper, every act of pride, every act of lust, every act of gluttony will be punished by death? Who believes that you can go to hell for any of these things, that a man can die not just physically, which separates him from people, but spiritually, which separates him from God? Who believes that it is that serious to do wrong and break God's laws? So hearts are hardened because people don't believe it any more. Yet God has said, "The soul that sins shall die." That is God's word.

But even more, we have had examples in our own world of God's fulfilment of that word. We have had a demonstration of his power to destroy. Where are the cities of Sodom and Gomorrah today? They are lying somewhere under the Dead Sea. The only thing that has ever been found of those cities is a graveyard and there is no other trace to be found. God has already shown that is what he does with a city that sins, and we do not take it seriously. We say, "That could never happen to us." Babylon is nothing but a heap of dust, and God has said it is such a wicked city that he will destroy it and it will be a place for jackals and hyenas to live – and we take no notice. I could give you any one of a dozen cities that God has wiped out for sin and we say, "It could never happen here."

So Pharaoh rejected God's words. He did not take what he said seriously. He did not take to heart the demonstration of God's destructive power and therefore his heart hardened itself against God and he refused to co-operate with Yahweh.

So we come to the second part of this study: having rejected God, retribution followed. There is an idea around, which I meet inside church as well as outside, that God is nice. I thank God for a Bible that does not use that word. What I mean is this: that God is so nice he wouldn't hurt a fly – that he would never punish anybody – and that is an utter lie. God is not like that. God is holy. When a man rejects God, God punishes that man. Make no mistake about it.

Three final punishments now come to Pharaoh, his family and his nation. We have seen how God hardened Pharaoh's heart – the first six times, Pharaoh hardens his heart, and the last four times, God hardens it. Now can you see what God does? God says, "Whatever path in life you choose, I will push you further along that path. If you choose to walk toward me I will draw you closer to me. If you choose to walk away from me I will push you further from me. If you choose to harden your heart against me I will harden it for you, if that is what you want." The worst punishment I can think of is to give people what they want.

There is a text in the book of Psalms I have never preached on, though I have often been tempted to: "He granted their requests and sent leanness into their soul." What a text! In simple English, God gave them everything they wanted and killed them spiritually. There could be no worse punishment for a man than to be given by God everything he wanted. It would kill him spiritually, and that is God's punishment for a man who hardens his heart.

It is, alas, a sad fact that two things will happen as I preach: either hearts will be more and more opened to believe in the God there is and to respond to him, in which case God himself will take their hand and draw them closer to him. Or their heart could close and say, "I don't believe in a God like that; I don't like to think of a God like that," and the result will be that God will push them further from him. "Today if you will hear his voice, harden not your hearts."

So if we are not careful, God will push us further down the road away from him as a punishment for not responding. This comes in the New Testament as well, lest you think I am way back in the Old. Let me read one text from Paul's letters, "They receive not the truth that they might be saved and therefore, God sends upon them a strong delusion to make them believe what is false." Do you understand that text? It is the same thing.

Why are people turning to false gods today? Why are they reading horoscopes more than they read their Bible? Is it a sign that God is saying, "You have chosen not to come to me for the truth? Therefore, I give you a spirit of delusion. I will let you go to these false gods if that is what you want. You want occult? You want spiritism? You want black magic? Then go and get it! That is my punishment for turning away from what I have tried to give you for two thousand years. It is only just and fair for God to do this; the punishment fits the crime.

Secondly: destroying Egypt's firstborn. I tremble when I read this. Can you imagine what it was like? I have lived in the Middle East, and I know that when a person dies, the whole household begins to wail. "Ahh, Ahh" – like that. You can hear it going down the street and it is a horrible sound. I remember hearing crowds of Arabs bewailing their dead like this over only one death. They are not like Westerners; they don't close in and hide their grief. They let everyone know that they are unhappy, and psychologically they are healthier for doing so because people come and mourn with them. Can you imagine what it would be like if the majority of the houses in your town had all lost someone by death and they were all wailing? You can hear it coming up the street, this cry getting larger and larger, coming nearer and nearer your house. What a dreadful experience. Yet, it was God's final punishment. Once again, it was just and I will tell you why: cast your mind back to the beginning of Exodus. Pharaoh had said, "Every Jewish boy must die," and God had given him nine opportunities to repent of that.

But when the tenth came, God said, "Pharaoh, you've done nothing but harden your heart. So what you said you would do to my boys, I do to yours." So every firstborn child died, every boy, the future hope of every family, for the firstborn son was the apple of his father's eye, the future of the family name, and even Pharaoh's own son who was going to sit on the throne of Egypt died that night. They all acknowledged God then, but they were too late. They realised that Yahweh is God then, but they had lost their children and they could not have them back again.

The third punishment that came was that in fact the riches of the Egyptians were handed over to God's people. What they had used for their own selfish purposes, their money, their gold, their silver, was handed over to the Hebrews. God can transfer silver and gold, all the silver and the gold is his. He can transfer it to God's people. I will tell you this: I don't care what title deeds people have to plots on earth, one day God will take all the earth away from selfish people and the meek will inherit it. He can take all the property in this world. "The earth is the Lord's and the fullness thereof" – that is carved into the stone above the main door of the Royal Exchange in London. The earth is the Lord's and he can give it to whoever he wishes. He has the title deeds to every bit of property and his final punishment to the Egyptians was to give their wealth to the Hebrews. Do you know what it was used for? It was used to build the tabernacle in the wilderness. The finance for that lovely place of worship came from the Egyptians to their Hebrew slaves.

What I am saying so far is this: if you do not co-operate voluntarily with God, you don't hinder God, you only hurt yourself. This is terribly important. When God said, "Let my people go," and Pharaoh said "No," that didn't hinder God, it only hurt Pharaoh. People who refuse to co-operate with God willingly will not hinder God, his kingdom is going to come, they will only hurt themselves, and that is the tragedy.

We had to take the first two points of rejection and retribution. It is only against that dark backcloth that the glory of redemption shines out. It is only because you face the stark fact that God punishes, that the blood of the lamb becomes wonderful to you. I know that people who only think of God as a nice old boy who never hurts anybody never talk about the blood of the lamb. They never thank God that he has passed over them; they do not have that in them. They don't know what redemption means because they don't know what damnation means. Redemption and damnation are two sides of the coin with God.

This wonderful word redemption can be defined by a text which in the Authorized Version is: "God put a difference between the Egyptians and the Hebrews." God made the difference between two lots of people. One lot suffered bereavement and death and the other lot suffered none. It was God who made the difference between them; it was not they who made the difference. God is putting a difference right through the human race at the moment. It is God's difference, not man's. The Hebrews were no better than the Egyptians. We are not told that God saved them because they were especially good.

In Deuteronomy God says to Israel, "Why do you think I loved you rather than the other nations?" The answer comes and it is a lovely answer, "I loved you not because you were great, but because I loved you." Do you understand that reason? God redeemed you, not because of anything in you that deserved it, but because he chose to show you his mercy—that is a lovely thought.

Why did he have all this business of the Passover? Why did he not just bring the Jews out and show them his mercy by setting them free from their chains and not have all this business about the lamb and the blood? Because they might have thought that they were better than the Egyptians and that they deserved to be released in some way. But God, by making them have a Passover lamb, taught them that they deserved his judgment just as much as the Egyptians. Do you remember that they had rejected his word in Moses? When Moses came they did not believe that God had come to set them free. They complained and they said, "We were better off before you came," and they told Moses to get out, as Pharaoh had done. But God was going to give them a chance to escape. At midnight one night, death would come. By rights it ought to have come to them. They deserved it as much as the Egyptians, having said no to him at the beginning just as they did. But Yahweh was going to give them a chance. He was going to tell them something they could do to avoid his judgments.

Now we come to this lovely story of the lamb – but it was a lamb a year old. It would have horns. It was a male in its prime not a little cuddly lamb. They must go through their flock until they had found one without any blemish, without a mark. They had to take that lamb and bring it into the house and it had to live with them for three days and it became a part of the family, like a pet. So they loved it and then they had to take the lamb and kill it. They had to do two things: they had to take its blood and sprinkle the doorposts and they had to take its flesh and eat it. So simple – now why? Why all this rigmarole of blood? Taking that branch of hyssop, dipping it in the basin and splattering the doorpost with it – why? Well the first thing that one could note is this: it was a sign to God. Have you ever tried to see the colour scarlet at midnight? It is one of the most difficult colours of all to see in darkness. If you have a maroon car, that is dangerous at night. Only God was going to see this. It was a sign for him. God can see blood at midnight. Whether it is light or dark, God can see everything. But here is the importance of the sign: when God came to that house and saw the blood he would say to the destroyer: it is alright, there has been a death already in that house; you can move on.

Do you see it now? I hope you saw it before, I hope you have lived with this as long as you have been a Christian. I hope you have realised this great message of the book of Exodus. Where God sees a life that has already been taken and blood that has already been shed he says: I can pass over that; the penalty has already been paid in that household; my judgment has already been exercised there – those people in that house will know how seriously to take my words and my judgment because they have had to take a life so that I might pass over.

The blood had already been shed. That ram was a substitute for a man in that house—a young man. Can you imagine what it would be like to be the elder son in a Hebrew house that night and to know that every other elder son was dying up the street? Then it came to your house and nothing happened. Then next door they began to wail and cry and you knew that the eldest boy there had gone and you knew that the only thing that had stood between you and death was the blood on the doorpost and that ram that had been killed.

That is how every Christian feels. There is only one thing between me and hell and that is the blood of the lamb of Jesus; there is nothing else between me and God's judgment. There is nothing else I can plead. I cannot say, "Lord I've tried to do good, I've never done anybody any harm," because that's not true. I cannot plead anything except the blood of Jesus Christ, and I can say to the Lord, "You can pass over me with your judgment because a lamb has died and the blood is already shed as far as I am concerned. Someone has taken my place, someone has died instead of me, someone bore your judgment instead of me, and therefore you can pass over me.

That is what it means to believe in Jesus. Not just to think he was a great person and that you like to know him and love him. It is to say, "His blood covers my sin." That's what it means to become a Christian. Not just to say, "I believe that Jesus lived two thousand years ago, he rose from the dead," but to say, "he died for my sin and he died in my place, he is the Lamb of God that takes away the sin of the world and my sin too," and you can pass over me God. You have a right to judge me; you have a right to take away my life because I have abused it and I have sinned with it. But you can pass over me; I am under Jesus.

Notice very carefully that they had to apply the blood to their house. It was not enough that the lamb had died. They had deliberately to take the blood and put it on their doorposts. If they had neglected to do that, then the angel of death would not have passed over. Though Jesus died for the sins of the whole world, and though anybody may come and claim the power of his blood, only those who apply it to themselves will find that God can pass over them. This is what forgiveness is. God says: I will pass over your sins; I will pass over the record – that is forgiveness. Only those who have taken the blood of Jesus will know that.

Do you realise that one day the destroyer will visit every home and every person in your town? The only thing that can save them is for them to take hold of Jesus' death and claim the blood of the lamb to protect them against the judgment of God. That is the blood of the lamb; it only needed to be done once, and they were free. It only needed to be done on that night and it was over. God had passed over and they could then know the mercy of God.

There was something else they had to do. After God has passed over them, they had to take then the flesh of the lamb and nourish themselves for the journey with it. What a profound truth here. It is not just the blood of Jesus once only, claiming that and knowing that God has passed over your sin. What follows? I will tell you what follows: you have started a journey, a pilgrimage, and you will need to feed on Christ every step of the way. You are going to need strength for the journey to take Christ within you, to nourish your soul on him and to feed on him. Then you can walk, then you can go out into the liberty that he meant you to have. You are not finished with the lamb when you have claimed the blood; you're going to go on feeding on him, the living bread, the Lamb of God.

So they took the lamb. With Christ it is all or nothing – you have all of him or nothing. They were told: you must eat all the lamb, nothing must remain. This is what I preach: when you have claimed the blood of Jesus and God has passed over your sins, then have all of Jesus. Nourish yourself on every bit of him, everything that he has for you. Feed on him; you have a long journey ahead, you are going to need everything of him in you if you are going to face it and get there.

Next, we think of "representation". That night was the beginning and the things they had to do represented so much of what lay ahead. I have a rather nicely coloured enamel plate that I bought in a little shop in King David Street in Jerusalem. It is a Passover plate; it looks like an hors d'oeuvre dish and that is precisely what it is. It has a little hollow for bitter herbs. That plate is used to represent the pilgrimage of God's people.

The first thing to notice about this feast that they were going to repeat is what they ate: unleavened bread. In the old days, they could not go out into the shops and buy yeast. Whenever they made bread, they kept a little bit of the bread aside and let it go mouldy – they let it ferment. When they wanted more bread, they took the old bread, which they call the leaven, and they put it in the new dough and then they left it to rise. Each time they would keep a bit of bread and let it go rotten and then use it to ferment the new dough. That is how they leavened their bread and made it rise.

God said, "Now tonight, no leaven." What did he mean? You are going to make a clean break; you must start feeding on new stuff now. You must not mix any of the old things you fed on with new food for my journey; you must start clean. Don't nourish yourself on the things you once ate when you were a slave. Which is why, in the New Testament, 1 Corinthians 5 goes on to say, "Since Christ, our Passover has been sacrificed for us, let us keep the feast with unleavened bread. Let's cut out the malice and hypocrisy and let's eat bread of honesty and honour and sincerity and truth." You see what a message this has for us—it represents feeding on things that are true and honest. Don't eat the malice any more in your conversation, don't eat the gossip anymore; eat the truth and the honesty and the sincerity— that is the food you're going to need. What about the bitter herbs? They remind the Jews of two things and they remind us of two things. First of all, of the bitterness of the life you left. You need to remember what God has saved you *from* to keep grateful: the lostness, the loneliness of life without God. But the bitter herbs were also to remind them that the journey to the Promised Land would be tough, it would not always be nice; it would sometimes be unpalatable. It is so with the Christian life: it is not always going to be easy and nice, it is going to be tough and hard. Getting to that

Promised Land in glory—bitter herbs.

Notice what they wore, ready for a journey. They were not sitting down for this. If you go to the Jewish Passover, they will stand around the table, overcoats on, walking sticks in their hands today, ready to go. When you start the Christian life, God is not calling you to sit in a pew for the rest of your life, he is calling you to walk: to be a Pilgrim. John Bunyan understood this better than anybody—that the Christian life is a journey until you get to glory and cross the Jordan River, until the trumpets sound for you on the other side.

You will never stand still, or you ought not to. You are going to journey every day nearer. You are on the march – don't ever think that now you have started the journey, now that you have had God pass over your sins, you can settle down. No, you are a pilgrim. They wore their shoes, their staff and their cloaks ready to go. God's people must be ready to go.

Then notice the time they took. They ate it in a rush. Got to eat it in a hurry; there is a sense of urgency. Procrastination is the devil's cradle in which he rocks sinners to sleep. What is procrastination? It is never do today what you can leave until tomorrow. It is to say, "There's plenty of time to start this journey." I remember talking to a man in a public house once; I was going from pub to pub talking about the Christian faith to anyone who would listen. We were having a kind of blitz of the town, a campaign. This man was about twenty-six and he said, "Look, when I'm middle-age and married and have got kids and settle down, I'll think of going to church then." He said, "While I'm young I want to enjoy life, there is plenty of time," but there isn't. You need to get going soon.

The lamb of the Passover was killed at three o'clock in the afternoon. We are told that in Exodus 12. The blood had to be on the doorpost at midnight, for God was coming. They had nine hours only between the lamb dying and the midnight judgment of God to get that blood over themselves. It is interesting that when Jesus died, he died at three o'clock in the afternoon. I don't know when God's midnight is. I don't know how far the clock of history has gone, but there is a midnight hour to human history.

Between the time of three o'clock of Christ's death on the cross and the midnight hour, which comes bringing death to all who have sinned, there is a limited opportunity to apply the blood of Jesus. Even if that midnight hour is not struck during our lifetime, there is a midnight hour to our life and we do not know when that strikes either. Death will come to us at some point. Therefore, they ate the Passover in haste. There is an urgency about this. There are people drifting through life thinking that any old time will do to get right with God. There is an urgency that needs to be remembered.

What the Passover is to the Jew, the Lord's Supper is to the Christian: a remembrance. People who had not shared in the original, Passover lamb were to be initiated into an experience of the Passover. Children were to be instructed, strangers were to be initiated. In Exodus, they were to be circumcised and brought within the people of God.

What is our task today? It is to bring everyone we can influence under the blood of Jesus. We must tell our children what the blood of Jesus can do. We must tell the strangers within our gates, if they will come, what the blood of Jesus can do, by leading them to Jesus Christ in faith. Let them come into the household which is under the blood of Jesus.

Whenever we take bread and wine, I think of the Passover of Christ; of the blood that was shed that God might pass over, the body that was broken and on which we may feed by faith and with thanksgiving: this is our Passover and it is repeated and will be until the end of the feast when we have that banquet with Christ in glory.

In 13:1 there is an instruction to consecrate all the firstborn to God. What applied to the eldest son in the Jewish community applies to all God's sons and daughters in the household of faith. If I am under the blood of Jesus, if I am only alive now because Jesus died on a cross, then I am his. I have no choice and my life must be dedicated to him. I do not belong to myself any more; when the blood of the Lamb has redeemed a life, that life belongs to the Redeemer.

READ EXODUS 13–15

If I were going to give a title to this study I would call it the day two and a half million people got baptised. For the passing of the people of Israel through the Red Sea corresponds (according to the New Testament) to our baptism in water. It came at exactly the point in their pilgrimage that baptism should come for us. They had already started the pilgrimage of the people of God; they had already believed in him. They had already put their trust in the blood of the lamb that God might not visit them with his punishment and with death. They were now set free from the wrath of God by the blood of the lamb and they had begun their journey to the Promised Land of blessing. But the thing that God wanted them to do now was to be baptised, and that is why he led them through the Red Sea. Read 1 Corinthians 10, where we are told that the story of the Exodus was written down for us. What is the point of our reading the history of the Hebrews? If we are not Jews, why read a bit of ancient history? According to 1 Corinthians, these things happened to them as an example to us and they were written for our warning.

Paul says that the people of Israel were baptised in the Red Sea. They went through the waters without coming to any harm. They went through a place where others would have drowned but they came through and they were baptised. So this study is really a study on baptism. After you have believed in the blood of the lamb, after you have started out on your pilgrimage, a decisive and final break is needed between you and the life you have lived.

For the people of Israel the Red Sea marked that break. It was the point at which they had their last contact with Egypt and with Pharaoh and with those who held them in their grip. It was their first real battle in which they stood still and saw what the Lord could do for them. It was a crisis. It was a crisis of leadership too. Moses was their God-appointed master and yet they had doubted his word. They whined and grumbled, right up to the Red Sea. But on the far shore of the Red Sea it says they were now baptised into Moses. In the same way, a Christian is baptised into Christ as we make our journey to the Promised Land.

Here they are setting out on their journey and the most extraordinary thing about this is the route that they took. If you can see a map of the Mediterranean Sea, find the Red Sea, a long, narrow strip of ocean which divides into two arms at the top, leaving a triangle of land which is the Sinai Peninsula, with Mount Sinai in the middle towards the bottom. Then, up to the right, there is a deep valley, a crack in the earth's surface which goes right down through the Great Rift Valley in Africa—the biggest crack in the Earth's surface, and this valley, heading north–south, fills up with water at one point. The Dead Sea, nearly two thousand feet below the Mediterranean, has no outlet.

The river Nile runs through the North African desert, creating a green fertile strip between Ethiopia and the Mediterranean. Opening out into this very fertile area there is the Nile Delta where the richest land is, and right there in that delta is the land of Goshen, where the people of Israel were put in the best land of all. But it was there that they became slaves and it was there that they built those cities with their slave labour and bricks without straw.

With that in mind we can consider the extraordinary route that they took to escape out of Egypt. The most obvious way, the quickest, the shortest and the most direct is to take the coast road to Canaan. That journey on foot would take less than two weeks and yet they did not go that way. In fact, they were to spend forty years on the journey. They need not have spent quite that long – they could have got there in months the way they took – but they so mistrusted God that they went a longer way round.

They went right down into the Sinai Peninsula, came up, nearly got into the land, went back down again, going across the Arabah as it is called, up the far side. The first question is: why did they go south instead of east and north? They went south and it says that God told them to. The reason was very simple: he didn't want them to be discouraged too soon by having to fight their way. This road was called, "the way of the Philistines" because it led to Philistia.

It says: "God did not lead them by the way of the Philistines lest they should be discouraged by having to fight soon after starting out." Now many have assumed that means that they would have to fight the Philistines a fortnight after leaving Egypt. But there is something more that we now know from archaeology which explains this whole thing. We now know that to protect their eastern frontier the Egyptians had a line of fortresses linking the Red Sea to the Mediterranean. The Hebrews would have had to fight their way through a heavily fortified line. It was, of course, primarily built to keep enemies out but it could also keep slaves in.

God in his mercy protected his people at the beginning from having to fight. They were going to fight later, but when somebody starts out on the pilgrimage that leads to glory, God has his own lovely way of protecting in the first part of the journey lest they be discouraged. I think all of us have known this. We became Christians and it was wonderful. It seemed as if we were enveloped in God's love. We felt invincible; we felt that even the devil could not touch us. God in his mercy gave us a honeymoon, a kind of period when, free from the battles and responsibilities, we could enjoy him. This is one of the reasons why he led them south.

The other reason was that he wanted them to have a decisive break with Egypt. He wanted to trap the Egyptian army so that they could never follow after them and take them back. If they had taken the way of the Philistines and even managed to break through the fortresses, the Egyptian army could always follow them through the desert. God was going to make this break and destroy the Egyptian army. He was going to do it through his own nature. He was going to use natural means to do it – he was going to use water to do it, and the route was through water.

I want to draw a lesson for you straight away: very often God does not lead you in what to you seems the most obvious, the most direct and the quickest way to reach your goal. Sometimes it is frustrating when God seems to be leading you in the opposite direction – when he seems to lead you in such a roundabout way that is going to take more time. We are in a hurry to get there and God deals with us more slowly. Happy are those who do what the Israelis did and they camped where God told them to go. They left their land, they went southeast, and they camped on the western shore of the Red Sea. They were obedient, and that led them straight into a cul-de-sac, a dead end. They found themselves in a place where they were absolutely hemmed in on three sides. If you can imagine that I'm facing south and I'm standing in the camp of the Israelis on that night. On my left is the Red Sea; straight ahead of me is a mountain range, the beginning of the Sudan Mountains—a mountain range that I can't climb over. To the right of me is the river

Nile and beyond that the Sahara Desert and God has said, "This is the way." You seem absolutely shut in. There seems no way out and then to my horror I turn around and in the distance I can see a cloud of smoke, dust getting nearer and nearer. Through the dust I can see horses and chariots and I am hemmed in at the back, absolutely blocked in. That is how they felt that night – utter catastrophe, utter despair, and they thought that having set out on the journey they would now never make it.

There comes a time in every Christian life where you get so shut in that you say, "It's impossible. I can't get out of this, I can't go forward; I am absolutely trapped. Right, left, forward, backwards—there is nowhere to go." Of course, when you are so preoccupied looking at all the walls around you, the best thing to do is to look up because there is nothing above you. The ground is down so you can't go down. Alright then, there's only one way out and that is to look up. But they didn't do this at first. They were in a dreadful situation. They did two things actually. They cried to the Lord but what did they cry? They whined to Moses and what did they whine? They said to Moses, "Why did you ever start us on this life? On this journey?" There are times when as a Christian you may want to say to those who led you to the Lord, "Why did you ever lead me into this life?" Of course, if you cry like that, three things have happened. Number one, you have forgotten the past. The Hebrews had forgotten God's mighty arm. Ten times he had sent a plague and now they are saying, "We'll never get out." Number two, they were fearful of the present. Fear of circumstances and of enemies takes away your love for God and your trust in him. You cannot be afraid and trustful at the same time. The third thing is that they were faithless for the future. It is incredible that having been able to see so many miracles they were now saying this kind of thing. They were saying to Moses, "Why did you bring us out?" John Bunyan in *Pilgrim's Progress* – a book that I hope you will read; if you haven't read it, please do so – describes how two people set out on the journey to heaven—Christian and Pliable. What a character Pliable is. As they set out on their journey they come to a marsh called the Slough of Despond. They get down into it and they get trapped in it. Their legs are caught in the mud. Pliable says, "I'm going to go back to where I was living, it's better than this struggle." There is a lovely character that comes into *Pilgrim's Progress* at this point. His name is Help. What a lovely name to have. That is all we know about this character in *Pilgrim's Progress*. He holds out a hand and helps Christian out of the Slough of Despond.

Sometimes if you are in the slough of despond you need a helping hand from another pilgrim; you need to go to another Christian and say, "Look, I'm depressed, I'm down; give me a hand, help me out." Well now, what is the cure for this kind of situation? Two things: stand still; go forward. Moses said, "Stand still," why? Where were they going to go? What else could they do? I will tell you where they were going to go. They were going to run back to the Egyptian army. They were going to go back and say, "Look we will come back as your slaves, just spare our lives." They were going to go back to their old life and come to terms. They were not going to run into the sea, they were not going to run into the mountains. They were not going to run into the desert – they were going to run back to Egypt. They were going to try to save their lives by grovelling in front of Pharaoh's army and saying: "Alright we'll come back, sorry. We didn't really mean to run away." The temptation when you are really in that kind of situation is to run, to panic, to go back to where you were, in the hope of saving something. Moses stood between them and the Egyptians and got them to stand still, not to run. Don't panic, don't go back to Egypt. Just hold on a moment.

There are times when you have to stand still, when you have to not move at all but to say, "God we'll just stand still until we hear from you what to do. We won't rush. We won't panic. We won't do what we want to do. We'll stay still and then we'll do what you want to do." Of course there is something in us that thinks we have got to do something about the situation instead of quietly saying, "I'll just wait right here until God tells me where to go." So they cried to the Lord and Moses told them just to stand still and to watch. He made them a promise: the Lord will fight for you. You won't even need to lift a finger. You just watch him. Get on with this situation and see what he can do in it. Then comes the moment when there is a command to move on. God now wanted the people to go forward.

These then are the two things you need to do when you are panicking in an impossible situation and you can't see the way out. Stand still for a moment to stop your panic, to stop running your way, then go forward in the way that God told you to go and see what happens. As you march up toward whatever seemed to block your way you will find it goes.

Pilgrim, in *Pilgrim's Progress*, saw two lions lying in the path, and he saw people running away from the lions and was tempted to run himself, but he was told, "Go forward." He walked up to these lions and they were lying in the path. Then when he got really near them he discovered that they were chained and that if he kept in the middle of the path they could not reach him. He went right through between their gaping jaws. It was quite a moment. That is what happens when you go forward—the difficulty that seems so impossible cannot touch you – go through and on your way.

Now let us look at the miracles that God did. First of all, there is the miracle of the dark sky. We are told that God made his presence visible among the Israelites – they could see him. What a comfort to them. I sometimes wish that I had had that experience. I have never seen God visibly present as a pillar of fire. I would imagine something like the mushroom cloud of an atomic bomb – by day looking like a gigantic cloud but by night seeming to burn and glow.

It is interesting that in warfare, in the ancient world, the commander in chief of an army would signal his presence in the field to his troops by lighting a bonfire so that they saw the flames and a pillar of smoke and they knew that the commander was in the field. Doesn't that make sense now? God is showing that he, the commander in chief, is right there and with them in the field. That is what they saw by night – this great glowing pillar – and by day this great cloud. He led them forward and he was in front of them.

Now the first thing that happens, when they stand still to see what he can do, is that he moves around behind them. God is not only our vanguard; he is our rearguard. He is not only in front leading us; he is behind, protecting us. He moved around behind and the cloud moved around the camp. Can you think of it moving around in the desert? We are told an interesting thing—that that night this pillar gave tremendous light to the Israelites and they could see where they were. But on the other side of the cloud it was pitch black. That is what God seems like to different people. To those who are walking in his way he is light, he illumines their path and shows them where to go. To those who are against him he is darkness and they see nothing.

The second miracle was, of course, the divided sea. Now I do not want to belittle this miracle and I don't want to explain it away but we are told in the Bible that God used natural forces to do this. I want to describe for you how that could be. In those days the map of the Middle East was slightly different from the map today in that the Great Bitter Lake, which is now in the middle of the desert between the Red Sea and the Mediterranean, was part of the Red Sea. A narrow neck of water joined the Great Bitter Lake to the Red Sea. I have interesting confirmation of this by way of a photograph of this whole area taken from an astronaut's capsule two hundred miles up. When you look at the Great Bitter Lake you can actually see in shadow the valley which was once filled with water and is now silted up. "Red Sea" is an English corruption of the actual name, which was "Reed Sea". Of course it isn't red. It was called the Reed Sea because of its shallowness and because reeds could grow at its banks.

So here we have the Israelites trapped by the Reed Sea. Now we are told not just that God divided the sea but that he sent a strong east wind. Why did the Bible mention that? It wants to tell us that wind is in God's hand in the song in chapter 15, and the sea was divided. The wind was seen as God blowing. We can see how this could happen and indeed in ancient Egyptian records there are three records of this happening. It is a very rare event. A strong east wind blew across the desert and the water moves in a westerly direction and almost literally piles up. This is the effect of the wind. If that coincides with an ebb tide in the sea, you see the two opposing forces are operating on the Reed Sea. The tide is pulling water one way; the wind is pushing the water, so you have a double pull. That not only pulled the water back but then the strong east wind blowing all night dried out the silt on the bottom sufficiently to walk on. This is the Bible description. We are not explaining away the miracle; we are saying what the miracle was. The miracle was in the wind and that is why the Bible mentions it. The wind produced the obvious result. But the marvellous thing is that God sent the wind at just the right moment – a rare event occurred just then. There is a tremendous sense of God being in charge.

When they got over, the third miracle took place – the miracle of the dead soldiers. The people got through dry but if it had remained like that, the Egyptians could have got through as well. If the sea had come back allowing the Egyptians to escape, I'll tell you what they would have done. They would have ridden around in their chariots at three times the speed of the Israelites—two and a half million men, women, and children on foot, they would have gone round the Great Bitter Lake and straight down after them down the western shore. It was essential to God's almighty purpose that he show the Egyptians "I am the Lord", and the water came back and the Egyptians were washed up dead on the seashore the next day.

I think we have got to have the right view of God here. According to Moses, he is described in chapter 15 as a warrior, and it was God who killed all the Egyptian army. That is the God we worship, the God of the Jews is the God of Jesus, and the God of Jesus is our God. If our idea of God cannot hold this and cannot contain the idea of a God who fights for us, then we are going to lack an essential part of our understanding of God.

We have been talking about redemption. The word "redeem" is used first in the Bible in these chapters. To be "redeemed" is to be set free, to be liberated, and to see those who have gripped you and held you, to see them gone forever. When you have been redeemed, one thing that will certainly happen, "Then sang Moses and the children of Israel." They sang the songs of redemption.

Christian praise was born in redemption and they sang, they looked. Now I don't know what you're going to think of this but they looked at all those dead bodies on the seashore and they sang and they danced. So would you if you had been a slave for 430 years, or you and your grandparents and your great-grandparents, and if you saw your tormentors dead on the seashore you would sing and dance. The song of Moses is a song of redemption. I want to examine this song and just analyse it briefly.

Notice the conditions that are essential for redemption hymns. Number one, deliverance – that you really have been set free; and number two, destruction – that your enemies have been destroyed. Think of the Hallelujah Chorus, which comes from Revelation 19, first mentioned there in connection with the destruction of human civilisation. When the smoke of the worldwide city Babylon goes up, men sing hallelujah. It is a "Praise the Lord" for destruction as well as deliverance. The two things go together. You can't be delivered unless your enemies are destroyed. Song comes out of the fact that Jesus is not only the deliverer but the destroyer. "Now is the prince of the world cast out," he said and that is why we sing about the cross. It was not only our setting free; it was the conquest of principalities and powers.

A song that springs form the heart, a redemption song, always has the double note of rejoicing that God has delivered and God has destroyed. Then you can really sing. It is only as you grasp these two things that you can really sing redemption. We are told in the book of Revelation that in heaven we will all sing the song of Moses, and the singing in heaven will be because of God's deliverance of us and the destruction of the world in which we have lived and which has been such a source of temptation, slavery and misery to us. How we will sing! Now, do notice that in the contents of this song there is a perfect balance. First, between the past and the future. God has brought us out of Egypt, he will bring us into his mountain Canaan. You can sing about two things: what God has delivered you from and what God has delivered you for; what he has brought you out of, what he is going to bring you into. So you can sing about hell and thank God for getting you out of hell; you can sing about heaven and thank God for getting you into heaven. Secondly, there is balance between the acts and the attributes of God – between what he does and what he is.

When we sing, it is not only of what God has done, it is of who he is. We praise God that he is a God of war and a God of peace – he is peace to us and war to our enemies. We praise him that he is light to us and darkness to them. That is balance. There is balance between his justice and his mercy and if you read this song both are praised. It is easier for us to sing of his mercy. It is not so easy to sing of his justice but we must do both. There is balance between the personal and the corporate, the songs that say, "I will sing of my redeemer" and those songs that say "We will sing of our redeemer." Praise is both and some of the hymns in our hymnbook are "I" hymns and some are "we" hymns—that is good.

Finally of course, the whole thing is drenched with glory to God. It is all about God; it is all to him. "I will sing of my redeemer." It is centred on him. It is not praising Moses. It is not praising the Israelites for having faith, it is praising God for leading them through, and our songs of praise must never praise men. The Bible gives the glory to God. Even Moses is not to be praised. "O praise the Lord the horse and rider went into the sea. Praise the Lord for he has triumphed gloriously." Then the ladies took it up and Moses' sister took it up and she started dancing. Why not? Singing and dancing becomes those who have been set free.

When the prodigal got home, the elder brother heard singing and dancing from the house. Why not? To dance for joy – you can only do that on the far side of the Red Sea.

READ EXODUS 16–18

When God brought the people of Israel out of Egypt he
didn't take them straight into Canaan. The milk and the
honey were waiting there for them but he led them through
the wilderness, and it is a pretty rough and barren place and
they had some very tough experiences there. Why did God
do this? For the same reason as he leaves us on earth after
we have become Christians. Why doesn't he take us straight
to glory? We are ready to go, we would love to go – it would
be so nice to step into heaven as soon as we were converted,
but he leaves us on Earth. From time to time our experiences
here are a bit of a wilderness, but the wilderness is where
you learn. This is where Jesus himself learned. We are told
in the New Testament that he learned obedience by the
things he suffered. Where did he suffer to learn obedience?
The answer is: six weeks in the wilderness after his baptism.

Christians may have a wilderness following their baptism.
They will have battles, they will have the kind of experiences
that Israel had in the few days after they went through the
Red Sea and were baptised into Moses. I want us to look at
six experiences they had, all of which are written down that
we might learn in the school of obedience to God. You learn
in the wilderness how to follow God's instructions and you
learn that when you follow God's instructions things work
out right. But when you follow your own thinking, things

go badly. That is a very hard lesson to learn but let us see how they learned it.

Let me sum up by saying this: they learned in the wilderness three things about God and three things about themselves. These are the two great lessons in the school of the wilderness: to learn what God is really like and to learn what you are really like. To learn how wonderful he is and to learn how dreadful you are. These are lessons that usually come as you go through the Christian life. They don't come at the beginning, it is as you go through the wilderness with God.

First of all consider the things you learn about God. You will learn first of all that he is there *with you*. His presence is a great thing to learn. It does not matter whether you are having a great time by the pools and palm trees of Elim or whether you are having a bitterly disappointing time at Marah, God is there and you learn that his presence goes with you every step of the way.

The second thing you learn about God is that he *protects you*. You need to learn of his protection in times of danger, in times of attack, so that when you face the enemy you trust God.

The third thing you learn about God is what we call his *providence*, which simply means that he is a marvellous provider. He provides everything you need at the time you need and just the amount you need – no more; no less. These are three wonderful things.

The three things that you learn about yourself are these: first of all that you are frail and that you are very weak. You will learn in the wilderness that you very quickly come to the end of your own resources. You learn in the wilderness that you are just not big enough to cope. Secondly, you discover the flesh. You discover the pull of Egypt—that is another lesson you need to learn and the Israelites learned it. Thirdly, you will learn in the wilderness your faithlessness – that God having helped you time after time after time, you can still get to the point where you doubt whether he is going to help you. You can still grumble, you can still complain.

Now every Christian could make a long list of times when God has helped them in the past, yet we are still tempted to grumble or complain. Consider human frailty, human flesh and human faithlessness, then put that together with God's presence, God's protection, and God's providence, and you have the answer.

Indeed you need to realize how low you are to find out how high God is. You need to learn how faithless you are to learn how faithful he is. In the grumbling and complaining of the people of Israel here, do you notice that God hardly rebuked them? He helped them! Is that not amazing? They grumbled that they had no water, that they had no food, and that they were having to fight, and that the way was tough. Yet God gave them food and water, and he fought for them. Think of the patience of God with us.

Now we outline various incidents that occurred in these three chapters. Ask God to bring it alive for you and speak to you again and help you to face life. Very quickly, after all the excitement of leaving Egypt and getting baptised in the Red Sea, they came into the wilderness of Shur.

There is a wilderness to be faced fairly soon in the Christian life. After all the excitement of conversion and the excitement of getting baptised, sooner or later you find yourself in a bit of a monotonous patch. The excitement is gone and things do not seem to be happening any more. There are no miracles to watch and you are just plodding on. The Lord takes you through the wilderness that you might learn to plod.

A plodding Christian goes places—far further sometimes than those who have a tearing hurry at the beginning and then they stop for a while and then they have another bit of a run and then they stop. Those who just go on plodding, walking the way of God, get places. Now they came into this place and it was dry, they began to run out of their water, it was monotonous and tiresome – the wilderness of Shur. Then in the distance they saw something they thought was going to be the answer and they saw some trees. They realised there was water and at first they may have thought it was a mirage, but as they got nearer they realised it was real. They came running up to the seemingly lovely pool and they drank from it, and it was found to be undrinkable. I know something of this because out in Arabia we drank water from artesian wells that came up through a natural deposit of Epsom salts. They came up terribly hot and they were undrinkable waters. I know the kind of thing that is referred to – full of minerals in the heat of the desert. After a monotonous, tiresome patch, this was a big disappointment.

Now I think every Christian has faced this kind of thing. Something they thought was going to turn out better than it did, something on which they pinned their hopes does not get fulfilled. They were going to learn a profound lesson about God. The lesson he gave was: this situation is perfectly alright provided you add to it what I will show you.

In this case, he told them to throw bits of tree into the water. It may interest you to know that the Arabs still do this. There are at least three trees of which they strip the bark and throw the bark into the water. I am told there is something about it causing the minerals to deposit or to "precipitate", to use the proper technical term.

Now if that is the explanation or whether it was a direct miracle and really had nothing to do with the tree at all but their faith in doing what God told them, I do not know. I only know that they needed to be shown by God how to put the situation right—that is all and that is the only lesson I want to draw from this particular incident, which is especially relevant when you have been going through a disappointing, tiresome patch and then some hope on which you have pinned your future collapses, and you could easily become resentful and bitter about it. The word "Marah" means bitter because the water was bitter, but the Israelites were bitter too. The whole situation was bitter and God told the people what to add to this situation that would sweeten it.

The interesting thing is that it was there at Marah that God gave himself a new name. He had already called himself, "I am", now he revealed himself as: "I am the God who heals". You will notice as they go through the wilderness to places like Elim no new name for God is given. Yet when they get to the disappointing places, the difficult places, the battles, it is then that they learn more about God. I will tell you this: that if your Christian life has been smooth, straightforward, simple and easy, then there are many names of God that you will not have got to know. But when you are really in trouble, when you are bitterly disappointed, when you are going through a bad patch, it is then that you discover more about God and he says, "I am the God who heals you." In fact, at that bitter place, the place where they felt the water was not even fit to drink God said: now look, you can drink it if you do what I tell you and I will keep you from all the diseases of Egypt if you just follow my instructions. In other words, you don't need to be afraid of drinking bad water. If you are following my instructions I will look after that side of it.

Clearly they were afraid that if they went on drinking it they would get disease. They had known what bad water in Egypt did, so they were afraid of disease and he says, "Follow my instructions and I am the God who heals. If I tell you to drink, it is alright." You know Jesus said something pretty startling. He said to his disciples, "You could take up snakes yet they wouldn't harm you." There are missionaries who can tell you that is exactly what God has done for them. In other words: if I tell you to do a thing, follow my instructions. They moved on from Marah and the next thing they came up to was a lovely oasis with seventy palm trees and twelve springs. Can you imagine it? After Marah?

There was an old lay preacher in the Shetland Islands, where I began my ministry, and he was a real character who once preached 82 sermons in one church – one on each of the springs and one on each of the palm trees. The congregation had to go through every spring and every palm tree here, and they found a meaning for every one of them. He knew what the word "Elim" meant, that is why. He had found the refreshment that God can sometimes give you. Maybe you have had a bad patch, gone through a dry period and had a bit of disappointment which, when handed to God, turned out right, and then quite to your surprise a bit further along there is a lovely blessing just waiting. We have all had our "Elims". The figures twelve and seventy are always very interesting. You find throughout the Bible (and I don't think I am reading too much into them) that twelve and seventy are the figures of God's ministry to people through people. He called twelve apostles. He sent out seventy, two by two. You get these two numbers associated with God sending the right people to do something. The spiritual meaning of Elim to me is that when you need it God will give you a ministry that will be so refreshing.

I have found that from time to time when I have been drained and when I have been needing help, God has led me to go and sit under a ministry that has been right for me. I have been ministered to. I have drunk from one of the springs. I have eaten the dates off one of the palm trees and it has helped me through. Thank God for the "Elims" of this life but you notice that they did not learn anything new about God at Elim. (I am not referring to any denomination today.) If you stay at Elim, if you stay at the place like that and say, "This is great, let us camp here, let us build houses here, we have enough to eat and enough to drink, let us not move on," then I am afraid that is as far as you will go in your knowledge of God.

God made no new revelation of his name or his nature at Elim. He just refreshed them and said "Now move on" – and they moved on. So from the place of delight they moved on and for the last time they saw Egypt on the far side of the Red Sea, for now they were going to turn inland. They were coming down the eastern shore of the Red Sea towards Sinai and at a certain point they would leave the coast and head inland through the wilderness of Sihn.

From the point of the coast at which they would head inland, they would catch their last glimpse of Egypt so it had a significance for them. They were now really leaving sight of the land that they had lived in. So they were thinking about all they had known there, and the food had been good in Egypt, even though they had to eat it in slavery. We are told about the garlic, leeks and onions and all the stew they had there. It makes your mouth water to read about.

Now they were leaving Egypt and its food behind and they found themselves in the wilderness of Sihn. The food was gone and they were saying, "Why did you bring us out Moses?" They were blaming Moses, and God said through Moses, "I brought you out, not Moses. You followed the cloud, not Moses. I led you this way. In grumbling against Moses you are grumbling against your Lord." Then God says: "I am going to give you not only bread, I'll give you meat too."

God has a way of providing not just the bare necessities but a table in the wilderness that has good things on it as well — meat. How could God provide bread and meat in the wilderness? This was a real miracle. I have worked out how much bread he supplied: something like forty and a half-million tons of bread in the middle of a desert! No one else has ever been able to do that. One way food came to them was of course the quails—little birds. Have you ever seen quails? Little birds running around, they migrate in thousands across the Middle East. At night they are exhausted with flying and they can only fly just a few feet above the ground, hopping a few yards at a time. Therefore they are terribly easy to catch, but the thing is on that very evening, for the first time, quails migrated that way through that valley and they came down in their thousands so that they had meat that night. In the morning they got up and they saw this little bread.

There have been attempts to describe it in natural terms such as honeydew or the excretions of the Tamerus tree, to explain this miracle. But the fact that it was God's miracle is proved by certain facts. Number one, there was exactly the right amount: three quarts per person. When they had gathered every bit off the desert floor, they had exactly three quarts for every person in camp, no more no less, and that is remarkable. God knew exactly how much to produce.

Secondly, there was twice that amount on the Friday morning. Nature doesn't do that kind of thing. Nature works on a seven-day week invariably, and I remember that from when I used to have to get up every Sunday morning at four and milk ninety cows before going to church. Yet here nature did something twice as great on Friday and not at all on the Saturday. Furthermore, the miraculous nature of this bread is seen in the fact that, six days a week, if they kept any till the morning it went rotten but on the seventh day when they kept it to the morning it was perfectly fresh. You can't get around the fact that God did this to keep two and a half million men, women, and children, and their animals, alive in the middle of a desert. It takes a big God to do that.

Now of course, we see great meaning in this because Jesus

himself gave us the key to unlock the meaning. He said: "I am the living bread" and, "I am the bread sent down from heaven." The people ate the bread in the wilderness and it kept them going another twenty-four hours but it did not keep them going forever. It couldn't. Sooner or later, even if they went on eating it, they would die. In fact, all but two of them did die in the desert even though they had the manna. But Jesus' teaching was: you eat me and you have got a life that will go on and on and on forever; I am the real bread you need. It was in the wilderness that the Israelites learned that man does not live by bread alone but by every word that comes out of the mouth of God – particularly the word that became flesh and dwelt among us. If you would know eternal life now and in the future, it will be by feeding on Christ the living bread. It is the only way, otherwise you are hungry in the wilderness. There is always a famine in this world for those who do not feed on Christ. Sooner or later you say, "I perish here with hunger and in my father's house there is bread enough to spare." Sooner or later you are dissatisfied with everything the world can offer, and sooner or later your heart cries out to feed on something else, and Jesus says: feed on me the living bread.

We move on now to the valley of Rephidim, and there they got thirsty. I suppose thirst is a good deal worse than hunger. Thirst is a terrible killer. They were in the valley of Rephidim thirsty – with parched dry lips. This can happen spiritually. I want you to be realistic, because if I do not tell you that there is a way in the wilderness for the Christian then you will be terribly hurt when you discover this for yourself. It is far better to know it now. You will get to the Promised Land but the way lies through the wilderness. There will be times when you are dry and thirsty—dry patches. Every Christian has known this.

How do you get through it? The same way they did there.

The people began to push God's patience to the brink. They were complaining and grumbling again. To tempt God is not to try to make him do something wrong but to try to make him do something right. Do not push God too far. Do not play about with his promises so that you doubt him so much that his patience comes to an end for you. Moses said that place was called 'Massah' – meaning testing God's patience, pushing God too far.

Then he took the rod that had done so much. It was only a shepherd's rod but then God is a shepherd, and he smote the dry red sandstone of the valley of Rephidim (you can go there today and see that valley) and he struck it. It cracked where he struck it and out gushed water. Not just a gallon or two, it must have been thousands upon thousands of gallons flowing across the desert floor. You can see them digging a pool so that it would fill up and the animals could drink; catching it in their pitchers so that they themselves could drink. The New Testament says in 1 Corinthians 10 that rock was Christ.

In other words, once again, if you are hungry then feed on Christ; if you are thirsty drink of Christ. He says that if you knew who you were talking to you would ask him for a drink. To the woman at the well who tried to laugh it all off with a joke, Jesus said, "I could give you a spring of water inside you welling up to eternal life." That is the answer to thirst. Why did Jesus say, "Blessed are those who hunger and thirst...?" Because they will then learn that God provides. They should be filled and if you have never been hungry for more of Christ and never been thirsty for more of his Holy Spirit, then you have not known what it is to be satisfied. But when you hunger and thirst and go to Christ with that hunger and thirst, then the Rock of Ages is all you need.

I turn away from these places where they had these experiences to two groups of people where they learned two more things. For the first time now, they received attacks directly from an enemy. The Amalekites had emigrated from Persia and had married into the tribe of Esau. The descendants of Jacob and the descendants of Esau were now to meet. One of the deepest tensions in the human race for about two thousand years was the tension between Jacob and Esau. It went down through their children and it went right down until, finally, from Jacob came someone called Jesus and from Esau came someone called Herod.

When Jesus and Herod met two thousand years afterwards, it was still Jacob and Esau meeting. Jacob is the man of vision and faith who lives for the future; Esau is the man who lives for the flesh and the present, who wants a plate of soup rather than a mention in someone's will. The Jacobs and the Esaus of this world are always in tension. There are those who see the future and live by faith in the future, and those who live for what they can get and enjoy now.

The battle between Israel and Amalek is the battle that will go on right through history between those who live for the next world and those who live for this one, and that is the battle that was there. Now we are told that the Amalekites began to kill off the stragglers. There is a sermon for you – the people of God who were lagging behind were the ones the Amalekites picked off one by one. It is vital that we keep up in the pilgrimage of life. It is vital that we keep in the people of God. It is those who drop out, the stragglers, whom the devil gets hold of. The Amalekites did not meet the Israelites head on, they came around the back and picked them off one by one.

So Moses rightly decided they must deal with this together. The fellowship must tackle this. The whole group of the people of God must meet them head on, and so came the big battle. In this battle, for the first time God said you must fight too. Remember how, when they had been fighting the Egyptians, God said, "Stand still and see what I will do for you." In the beginning of your Christian life God will fight your battles for you, but later on he expects you to fight. It is part of growing up. But two things are needed: a sword and a rod.

You notice that the young men went down into the valley with swords and the old men went up the hill with a rod. This is a picture of the people of God tackling a situation. Those who are able go into the front line – older ones, up on the mountain, praying for them. This is the right way to tackle a spiritual battle. Older members, do you realise how important your task is in the church of Christ? Even if you cannot come out to services any more, do you realise that you can be up the mountain holding up Moses' hands? That is where the old men were. They were old men up there – Aaron was old, Moses was old – and they were up there holding up the rod of God, praying for those down below in the front line.

The whole people of God operates together. Young men in the front line get on with the job, the older ones are praying for them. You notice that as long as Moses' hands were up, the battle went up, but as soon as the hands began to flag it went badly. So more help was needed and his hands were held up by other people. What a picture of prayer and intercession for the battle in the frontline. This is the combination. Here is a lesson they learned: that God expects us to fight and we fight both with the sword in the practical way and with the rod in the prayerful way. I understand this to mean that prayer is hard work. I don't think it is right that you should only pray when you feel like it. Prayer is work – you roll your sleeves up spiritually and get down to prayer. If you cannot think of what to say then you think hard and ask the Lord what you should say.

You can get tired in a prayer meeting and Moses got tired,

yet the others held him up, encouraging him to go on praying until the battle was over. How long should you pray about a problem? Not just once, twice, but until it has gone. Then you see in the battle when you have won the battle, when the prayers have been answered, and you are through – you have found out something more about God. You have found a new name for God: *Yahweh Nissi*, which means God is our banner, which means God is our emblem as it were. When the banner comes into the battlefield, the enemy sees that and runs. Do you know *Yahweh Nissi*?

Finally, there was something that was necessary within the people of God. They had won their battles with enemies outside, but they were now losing the battles between themselves. Bear in mind that here were a lot of people who had been slaves and always told what to do by someone else. They were now free and they were now, as it were, able to do what they wished. The result was that they were crossing each other. They were arguing. The people of God having come into the freedom of God were now disputing with each other.

Moses was trying to keep them all happy. He was the pastor, the leader, the captain of this great number. He was trying to settle every question that arose among the people of God. He had a pastor's hour that lasted twenty-four hours a day apparently, or at least from morning to evening every day. His father-in-law Jethro got worried about it. Now there are some lovely touches. I can see why he first got worried about it (his daughter getting no attention, no family life). Jethro came and pointed out that this was silly. Moses would not only wear himself out, he would wear the people of God out and they too would suffer. They were hanging around all day to try to see Moses and that would not help. It meant that some things were not getting dealt with as soon as they should. Disputes could grow, misunderstandings snowball.

Moses would have to do something about this.

Moses listened to his father-in-law (not a bad thing to do sometimes). He took advice and he took it to the Lord. Moses tackled the basic problem of how to keep all the people of God happy with one another. He realised that one man could not possibly do it. That this was simply letting situations go by the board and go too far. So what did he do? When I realised what he did, I'm afraid I laughed out loud. I found it so funny. He appointed over seventy-eight thousand people to do his job – one for every thousand, one for every hundred, one for every fifty, one for every ten, and so on. So clearly he had been a bit overworked.

Every ten people would then have someone to look after them pastorally, and that is a very sensible arrangement because ten people can always feel they have someone they could get hold of immediately if one person has only ten. But then he said that those people who each have ten to look after should have someone to look after them, so he appointed one over every five of them. So there were fifty people at the bottom, then five people looking over them, and one person looking after those five. You got the build up, and then hundreds, and then thousands, and finally Moses. He needed about five levels in that little pyramid to cope adequately with the numbers.

On the same basis, a church I led would have needed a pastor, elders, and pastoral visitors each with ten, and an elder with five pastoral visitors. That is the kind of thing and you can work it out for your situation, so that everybody can get straight through to someone with their needs and then, if the needs are complicated or deep, they can be passed on. Moses was teaching what God's laws were and when an individual needed to work out how to apply it they went to their captain of ten. If the captain of ten said this is a bit too much for me then they went on to the captain of fifty, and so on. What a sensible arrangement.

I can guarantee that some of the old Israelis would have said: "Well I always got through to Moses with my problems and Moses hasn't been to visit me since we had elders." Can you see that being said? But it was sensible and Jethro was absolutely right. The harmony of the people of God would suffer if it remained a one-man band. He was absolutely right because things would not be dealt with as they should be, and so with divine common sense he set a pattern which I think we would do well to take heed of today – and in this way things went right.

Jethro was a very sensible, godly man who rejoiced in everything that God was doing for his people, a man who was pleased with his son-in-law, glad to hear of all that God has done through him and for him. But he never got to the Promised Land. He was a man who never left Egypt either. He was sympathetic, he rejoiced in what God was doing, and was glad to have a daughter of his married into such a people, and yet he never fully identified himself with the people of God and never went along with them. He was a man who comes into the story and goes out again.

He was such a sensible and helpful man. You know, one of the difficulties or tragedies there is in every church are the men who are glad that their children come to Sunday school, that their wife is a member, and they are glad to hear of all that God is doing and the people he is helping and saving, yet never fully identify, never get right into the people of God. The tragedy is that when Canaan is reached, those men might not be there. God grant that the Jethros of this world may become part of the people of God and walk with them through the wilderness and across the Jordan into the land flowing with milk and honey.

READ EXODUS 19–20

There are two ways of learning in life. One is experience and the other is teaching. One is through acts and the other is through words. Now experience is a hard school but fools will learn in no other. Wise people learn from teachers. God was wanting to teach his people the right way to live. He took them to a wonderful sanctuary with a pulpit that he himself had made. Now I'm going back to the map. The people of Israel were travelling down the east coast of the Red Sea. Mount Sinai however lies in the middle of the peninsula, not right at the end. So they cut straight across the peninsula along a valley, which cuts straight through from east to west. Halfway along you come across the most amazing place called the *raha* which is the Arabic today for the palm of the hand.

This place has a large plain two miles long, half a mile wide, almost perfectly flat and made of sand. At the far end of the plain from which you enter there is a gigantic mountain, thousands of feet high and it comes straight down into the plain. It is like a wall at the end. It is a marvellous pulpit, and there is an encircling line of hills around the plain, and the acoustics are such that somebody up the mountain talking can be heard right around the plain. It is a remarkable place. Someday in the distant centuries, way back when the earth was still being moulded, God made that place as a sanctuary for his people and he built a pulpit at the end of it for himself.

He was going to teach his people from that pulpit. I have seen photographs and maps, but I would love to go and see that pulpit. What a place it must have been! They came and they camped, two and a half million of them and their animals, in that whole plain.

It must have been quite a crush as they were together looking up at the mountain. It never has been a volcano. Yet what had happened to Moses with a bush was going to happen now with a mountain. When Moses saw the bush he saw it burning with flames, yet the bush was not touched. But only one person can see a bush on fire, and so God, desiring to impress all of them with his presence, set a whole mountain shaking and burning with smoke and flames. There is no trace today of those flames on the mountain. Like the bush it was not touched. But the fire of God came down upon it. The fire was not in the mountain but in God. That was really the meaning behind this mountain that some have said was a volcano.

You could say that the book of Exodus splits into the first twenty chapters and the second twenty. This passage is the kind of watershed of the book. Everything builds up to Mount Sinai and then flows down from it. I could give two titles to the first twenty chapters and the second, which would sum it up simply: *trust and obey for there's no other way*. Indeed the first twenty chapters are how God taught his people to trust, and the second twenty chapters are about how he taught them to obey. That is why the first twenty chapters are rather more exciting than the second twenty. It is always more exciting to trust God's mighty acts than to learn to do your humdrum acts. It is always easier to trust than to obey.

But now we are going to see that we trust and we obey if we are ever to get to the Promised Land. You must trust God to save you, but then you have to work out your salvation – the salvation that God has worked in. God has saved you but now work it out in fear and trembling. This is the message of both the Old Testament and the New. You have trusted him for salvation, now obey him for blessing. So we have this picture, and Exodus is almost a mighty mountain leading right up to the point of the Ten Commandments and then flowing from it.

The two things that God wanted to preach about from his own pulpit were these: the holiness of God's person; the holiness of God's people. These are the two great truths you need to learn if you are going to obey God. It is not easy to obey God. You need a motive to obey God. You need some kind of stimulus to do so. The answer is to be found in realising God's holiness. Then and only then will you learn to obey.

Let us look at the first lesson: the holiness of God's person. We all need to learn that there is between sinful man and a holy God a barrier, because we are so different from each other. There is a fence between us, and so God instructed Moses to put up a fence so many yards back from the edge of his pulpit. No man and no animal must get through that fence. God is not to be tampered with. He is not to be played around with. He is not to be putty. God is a holy God. Our God is a consuming fire, and fire is something you respect. You put a fireguard around your fire. Fire is not to be played around with but to be respected – and you teach your children to respect fire.

Our God is consuming fire and it is the New Testament that says, "It is a fearful thing to fall into the hands of the living God", not the Old Testament. For our God is fire. Now they were taught this lesson by the fence, by being told keep away from God's pulpit. Don't get overfamiliar. Have a healthy awe and respect for God when he is talking. Don't try to get near to see. Don't try to get over-curious. God will tell you what he wants you to know. Let him speak to you. This is the healthy reverence we still need. I had been speaking at a meeting where there were some three or four hundred people. We felt God's presence – terribly real. I said "Let us pray" and one man wrote to tell me afterwards that he saw tongues of fire on each of our heads. God came down. That fills you with reverence and awe. You don't want to play about with a God like that. You don't want to be over-familiar or cheeky to a God like that. You are left in wonder, love and praise, in worship and awe. God could touch you with fire now without a hair of your head being singed, but God is real. The thunder, the lightning, the smoke, the shaking of the mountain – it was all designed to impress those people that God is holy.

Furthermore, there was the fact that they had to have a mediator to go to God for them – somebody who was worthy to go, somebody whom God had chosen. We need a mediator with God. Not one of us has the right to come straight to God. We just don't have the right, but thank God that in the Old Testament as in the New, God provides a mediator — in their case Moses. The law was given through a mediator. In our case there is one mediator between God and man – Jesus Christ. He will go for us. Every prayer we offer to God the Father must go through Jesus our mediator because God is holy and I have no right whatever to offer my prayer to God except through Jesus my mediator. So the mountain and the mediator together said: "I'm holy, keep your distance."

Three times God said that and Moses said, "Look you don't need to keep telling the people this. You've said it once." God said, "Go and tell them again." One of the things we need to be constantly reminded of is that God is holy and he is not to be played about with but to be taken very seriously indeed. We need to be reminded of that for in the glorious joy and peace that we have in approaching him boldly now through Jesus we can forget his holiness and we can get too familiar unless we are very careful. So God said: go down, go down; go down, a third time. He was to keep telling them: don't come near.

The other thing that happened was of course the fear of God. Fire produces fear. It is bound too. Indeed if you saw a fire you would have fear. But the fear that the people had was a wrong kind of fear. They were all up against the fence in the beginning and then God spoke and they all ran to the other end of the plain. They said to Moses, "Don't let God speak. You tell us what he says but we don't want God to speak directly. You tell us what he says." Now that is a wrong kind of fear. It comes up whenever God speaks directly in a fellowship. People much prefer preaching to prophecy. Why? Because preaching is a man telling them what God says; prophecy is God speaking directly. That is why the gifts of the Spirit sometimes cause real fear when people are prophesying or giving a word of wisdom or knowledge or speaking in tongues because God is speaking. People say: I would much rather have the preacher tell me what God says – I don't like God speaking – that is too near to me; it is God getting a bit too near the bone.

But we must be ready to let God speak to us. That is not what we should be afraid of. What we should be afraid of is what Moses says: "God came to you in this way so that from now on you will be afraid of sinning against him." That is the fear of God – not the fear of God speaking directly to me but the fear of disobeying what he says; not the fear of God drawing near to me but the fear of me running away from him. Do you see the right kind of fear? There is a fear of the Lord that is the beginning of wisdom. It is not being afraid of God getting near to you, it is being afraid of your not wanting him near. So if God speaks to us in a service in a more direct way than preaching we should not fear that. We should fear whether we are ready to listen and to obey.

Having learned the lesson of the holiness of God, the Israelites could now learn the lesson of the holiness of God's people. I like to think of this whole scene at Mount Sinai as a wedding service. That is what it was. God had rescued them from slavery in order to marry them in order to have a vowed covenant. It is a wedding service taking place now in front of God's pulpit. The people of God, the bride of God, are going to be married to God and are going to undertake certain promises: I will. A marriage always has a covenant at the heart of it and a covenant has certain vows and promises at the heart of it. This was God's marriage with his Israel. Having set them free to serve him he tells them what promises they will have to make.

I find it a very solemn duty to marry two people and I am more nervous in a wedding than in anything else I do because of its solemnity, seriousness and possibilities. You realise the meaning of these words more and more fully: "for better, for worse, for richer, for poorer, in sickness, and in health till death parts us". Israel is going to marry God now in front of his pulpit and here are the promises: You shall have no other gods before me; you shall not make any graven images; you shall not take the name of the Lord your God in vain; you shall give one day in seven to him; you shall honour and respect your parents, and so on.

What God is saying is this: I did not set you free from Egypt in order to let you do what you want; I did not redeem you to be free to do anything you like; I set you free to serve me – to be governed by me instead of being controlled by the Egyptians; now you are coming under my will.

God does not set us free from sin in order to be free to sin. He sets us free to serve him. So he tells us the terms of his service. Therefore let me say now that the people of God are not meant to be a democracy – government by the people. They are not meant to be an aristocracy, government by the few. They are not meant to be an autocracy – government by one man. They are meant to be what is called a theocracy and that means government by God. Therefore the idea of a church as a democracy in which all the members have their say at a church meeting is just not on; it is not biblical.

The idea that the church is to be governed by bishops or anybody else in an autocratic manner is not on, it is not biblical. There is only one form of government for the church of Christ and that is theocracy – God telling his people what to do. At a meeting for the members of a church we are not interested in anyone's view at that meeting, we come together to pray that God, using our mouths, will speak to each other as to what his will is and what he wants us to do in the church; what he wants to do with us as a people.

Now let us look at these Ten Commandments. He has told them of course before the wedding to keep away even from their own wives that they might come to him with all their affection on this occasion. He has told them to wash their clothes. I think that is the only biblical basis I can find for getting dressed in your Sunday best. But I think if you were meeting the Queen you would not come to her in dirty clothes. I don't think you would turn up for your wedding in dirty clothes. You come in the cleanest clothes you have. We are not saying "Sunday best" now, we are saying that somehow putting on clean clothing on Sunday is expressive of a frame of mind that says God is holy. It is expressing your inner feelings. So they came ready, in washed clothes, with all their affection for the wedding.

The source of these Ten Commandments is in revelation. Moses did not think them up, God gave them. Some scholars have pointed out that there are some similarities between the Ten Commandments and other laws of that time. For example, Hammurabi wrote his laws and some of them are the same. People say that Moses was just sort of picking up laws from all over and putting them together and copying others, but that is not true. Why are the other laws the same as Moses in some cases? The answer is very simple: these are God's laws written into human nature, written on man's conscience. God gave them to other men too in their conscience.

In fact we are told in Romans chapter 2 that those who have never heard the Ten Commandments know some of them written on their conscience. Isn't that amazing? Why? Because these are not arbitrary laws. This is how we are built. You can find out the rules for running a car in two ways. You can either get the maker's handbook and read them, or if you are clever and mechanically minded you can study the car itself and you can say well obviously that is how it has got to work. You can tell God's laws either from reading the Bible or from studying your conscience. The fact that other men read their conscience more or less correctly does not mean that Moses copied them. God gave these laws.

But there is one difference between, on the one hand, the laws of God, and on the other hand, all the laws of men, of Hammurabi, and everybody else including the lawmakers of England today. Human laws begin like this: if you do this then the punishment will be that. They begin with the word "if", whereas divine laws begin "thou shalt not". Have you noticed that difference? Human laws are casuistry. They say if this then that, and all the laws of Hammurabi are if you kill then your life will be taken. If you steal, then so and so will happen. God simply says: you shall not. In other words, here is an absolute basis for morality.

There is an eternal difference between right and wrong and God has set it. He does not argue and discuss with us. He is saying this is it, here is the line I have drawn: you shall not. It is as simple as that. We live in an age of discussion and dialogue and everybody who says anything must face a panel on TV and have questions thrown back at them. But God's Word is not to be modernised or debated. Its source is revelation. God says: this is the way, walk in it. I am not going to debate it with you. I am not going to argue whether adultery is out of date or not. I am not going to argue about stealing or pilfering, or what have you. I am not going to argue about these things. You shall not. God gives us from his pulpit, his laws. He has written them on consciences but the clearest writing of all is right here.

The second thing about the Ten Commandments is that the basis is *redemption*. Do you notice that God did not give the Ten Commandments to the children of Israel in Egypt? He saved them first and then said: now walk this way. He said I am the Lord your God who brought you out of slavery, now serve me. God in his gracious mercy says: get saved first and then walk right. Don't let it be the other way round. That way is legalism. God does not say: keep my commandments and I will save you. He says: I will save you, now keep my commandments. In other words he wants grace first and gratitude second. He wants love first and law second. He wants salvation first and service second. One of the greatest misunderstandings of Christianity in our land is that you get good first and saved second; that you keep the commandments first and then you will get to heaven. It is the other way round. God has said: I have brought you out, now keep my laws. The basis is redemption for the simple fact is that until God has saved you, you will never keep the Ten Commandments. Until God has redeemed you, you won't love him enough to do it because love is the fulfilling of the law.

The third thing to note about every one of these ten "words" as they are called in the Bible, the principle is reverence or, in simple modern English, respect. Man shall not live by bread alone but by every word that comes out of the mouth of God. Respect God, respect his name, respect his day, respect his infinite character that cannot be expressed in an image; respect your parents and respect your neighbour, respect his life and property and marriage and reputation. That is the one thread that ties the whole lot together. A man who respects is a man who loves. Love respects.

The Ten Commandments in detail are fairly straight-forward though I would point out here a few things in them. God says that when he has to punish a person for breaking the commandments the effects of that punishment will last for at least four generations. Now that seems to some people terribly unjust. I am afraid it is simply true to life that what parents do goes on down through the generations. Their influence is bound to last. Keep the commandments and God's love goes down through the generations indeed. I reckon you can live on spiritual capital for four generations. Then it runs out. We have seen this in Britain. We are now some generations of people away from God. The last traces of Christian morality are going. The last traces of belief in God are going. They have managed to live for three to four generations or more without God and they have lived on the spiritual capital of their great-grandparents but it is going rapidly now. You see, the great mass exodus from churches of Britain took place in the First World War. That is when it happened. Now we are asking why society is like it is. It is because we have been living on spiritual capital and we are getting bankrupt. That is the real economic crisis. On the other hand, someone who loves God and keeps his commandments is going to have a sweetening influence on the next three generations, but someone who doesn't is going to have a bad influence on the next three. We cannot live as isolated units. We have got neighbours we influence. We have got descendants we influence. We influence those who come after us. So God gives us these words not only for us but for our children and our grandchildren and our great-grandchildren.

Here are a few further brief points about the Ten Commandments. First, notice that, in God's plan, duty to God comes before duty to your neighbour. The same with Jesus: Love the Lord your God with all your heart and soul and mind and strength, and love your neighbour as yourself. How many people think that Christianity starts with loving your neighbour? It does not. God's plan for people is that they start by loving him. A person is a sinner if he doesn't love God, no matter what he does for his neighbour. It is loving God first then you love your neighbour.

Secondly, I want you to notice that the Lord said love will keep them all. You can squeeze all ten to two. Love God, love your neighbour and you have covered them all. Then he said I'll give you a third: love one another. But it is all love from beginning to end.

Then I want you to notice that if you break one commandment you have broken the whole thing. These are not ten separate commandments. They are pearls on a string. The string is respect and love and they all hang together and James says in his letter if you break one you have broken the lot. What happens when you break the thread of a necklace of pearls? You lose them all and you are scrabbling about trying to pick them up again. It just needs to be broken at one point. This pattern of God's will for us is a single thing, ten facets of a beautiful character and love and respect and you may have kept nine out of ten but you have broken the Ten Commandments. You have broken the law. To break the law is to break a link in a chain of respect and the chain is useless. It is important to remember that they belong together.

Then I want you to notice this: the Ten Commandments tell me something dreadful about my heart. They tell me that I need to be told this. What a comment on human nature.

Human nature needs to be told to reverence God. Human nature needs to be told not to talk falsely about others. Human nature needs to be told to respect father and mother. The tragedy is that the Ten Commandments are the greatest indictment of the human race there has ever been – that they were necessary. God is telling the people of Israel: this is what you do and this is what you must not do. He is giving us a picture of sin in these laws. He is telling us: this is what you are like.

If you think that that is a bit harsh, then let us dwell on the tenth commandment. Paul said, "I kept the other nine but when I got to the tenth I finished." You shalt not be greedy or envious of things that other people have. It is the only commandment that is concerned with how you feel rather than what you do. No human court could ever take you to court for coveting. Can you imagine what it would be like if that was written into our law books – you shall not covet – and you were having to stand in dock and your counsel for the defence was trying to defend you, and counsel for the prosecution was trying to prove that you had coveted? Do you know that King Alfred did write that into the English law, but they have never been able to find a way of applying it? Only God can charge you with coveting. He will. Paul said: when I read the tenth commandment I find all manner of coveting in my heart. The law killed me dead because I had broken the whole thing by being greedy and envious

Returning to my main points, consider the effect of the Ten Commandments. It is reward: a special relationship to God. You will be my peculiar treasure. It is a special function in the world. It is a special character: you will be a holy nation.

What a reward. For keeping the commandments the reward is that you are a special treasure to God. You have a special function to the world and a special character among the nations.

Finally, the object of the Ten Commandments is reliability. God wants reliable people. The whole object of giving us his law is that we might be reliable – people who can be trusted with property, not to steal it; people who can be trusted with others' reputations, not to ruin them; people who can be trusted to honour their parents – reliable people, because respectful people are reliable people and God wants reliability.

The Lord tells us what to do and I know that those Ten Commandments are right for me. I know that I need winding up once a week spiritually and physically, yet that does not help me to do it. I know what is right and yet I do what is wrong. That is the tragedy of the Ten Commandments. In Romans 7 Paul says: I know that the commandments are holy and right and good, but as soon as somebody tells me you shall not, I want to do it. As soon as somebody tells me what I must not do I have a desire to go and do it. You can test this desire. Put a young teenage boy into a library with all the books that he could possibly ever want to read on every subject in the world and put one book in that library not to be read by anyone under twenty-one. Leave him alone in the library – that is what the law does. In the college that I attended at Cambridge we had one undergraduate who put up on his study door, a notice – "Silence I'm studying." You can guess what we did. Human nature, when told not to do something, goes straight away and does it. The worst of it is the law not only tells me what not to do it gives me an actual desire to do it. There is something in our nature that actually wants to do anything that is wrong to get a kick out of it. Therefore God's law failed. Those Israelites broke every one of those Ten Commandments afterwards. Something more was needed than law because every one of us has broken the law and the law damns every human being. As soon as you read the Ten Commandments you are damned by them, especially if you read Jesus' version of them in which he applies them to your thoughts and feelings.

So what is the answer? There was two thousand years ago a man born who was the Son of God and he was born a Jew and he was born under the law and at the age of twelve he took upon himself the responsibility of keeping those laws and he kept every single one. For all his life, every day, he gave God the Father for the first time in history a life that served God in every detail. He kept that law to the letter. At the end of his life, which was not very long they condemned him under the Law of Moses to death. The curse of breaking the law was put on Jesus. In Galatians 3 Paul says that the curse of the Law of Moses is in these words: "Cursed be he who does not continue in all of them to do them." That curse was put on Jesus for cursed is everyone who hangs on the tree. The amazing thing is that the law, which condemned us, was fulfilled in Jesus perfectly and he took the curse into his own perfect will and body and he suffered. Law came by Moses but grace and truth came by Jesus Christ. That is the difference. We don't live *under* the Ten Commandments any more. We live *by* them but not under them. We want to keep them because we love God but we are not under the curse any more. They don't damn us any more. They say "you shall not" and we say "Lord, I don't want to any more". God in his mercy has found a new way. Let us rejoice that Christ has redeemed us from the curse of the law, brought us into a new covenant based not on keeping the commandments but on confessing our sins. That is the basis now. It is based on the new covenant of forgiveness in which God says: your sins I will remember no more. I am going to forgive now and I am going to bring you into a new covenant with me. The wine in Communion is a symbol of the blood of the new covenant shed for you and for many for the remission of sins. That is better than they heard at Mount Sinai. We heard it at one of God's other pulpits—Mount Calvary—a mountain on which Jesus died. So we have come right to the cross. We have not come to a mountain that is burning with fire and smoke. We have come to the heavenly Zion, those who have been washed in the blood of Jesus, and to the New Jerusalem, city of the firstborn.

READ EXODUS 21–24

Both Christianity and Judaism are religions of a book. Some accuse us of what they call "bibliolatry" meaning Bible worship. We plead not guilty to that charge. We do not worship the Bible, we don't kiss it, we don't bow down to it, we don't say prayers to it. We don't fall down before it as a graven image. We are not "bibliolaters", we don't worship a book, but our religion is based on a book and I will tell you why.

We believe that the God who made the universe is the God who talks. He has spoken to people. Those who have heard him at the time know what he said, but how are subsequent generations to know what God has said? The answer is that it had to be written down and passed on. From the very beginning of God speaking, his words have been written down in a book and we have it in the Bible. This is not the book of the ideas of Moses and Paul and Elijah and Isaiah. This is the book of the words of God and is to be approached in that way. From these words you get a wonderful picture of what God is really like, how he feels about what happens on Earth, how he feels about that argument that you had with the neighbour over your fence. We know what God thinks about little things like that from these chapters. The Psalmist says, "Oh how I love your law. I meditate in it day and night." Do you meditate in this law? Do you love this law? Do you love to see the care and the interest and the concern of God expressed in the book of the covenant? For when the Psalmist said "Oh how I love your law" he meant the law that came through Moses and we are to love that law. We are to meditate in it until we think the same way as God about people and property, relationships, and all the matters that we have looked at.

Of course, the laws he gave to them were suited to the agricultural community. For example, he talks about the owner of a bull and the bull goring someone and killing them. If he were talking today or if God were giving us the same law today he might talk about our dogs. If you knew your dog to be dangerous then God will hold you responsible for the behaviour of your dog, but the principle is the same. The principles of these laws are the laws of God, and we need to learn them and meditate upon them and say: what is God getting at here? The first part of the passage is called the book of the covenant. It lasts from the beginning of chapter twenty-one through to chapter 23:19. This was probably the first part of the Bible ever to get written down. For Moses there was getting the ten words of God and the amplification of them. He came down from the mountain and recited them all from memory. The Holy Ghost can do wonders with a person's memory when he is passing on the Word of God. Jesus promised that to his own disciples. He will bring all things that I have said to your remembrance. Then, having recited them, Moses spent the whole night writing them down so the next morning he had that to show them. So when they vowed obedience to God they did it on that writing. A survival of that is in law courts today when people swear on the book to tell the truth, the whole truth and nothing but the truth. Our loyalty to God depends on a book. You cannot say, "I believe in God but I don't believe this book." You cannot be loyal to God without being loyal to his words, and that is why the Bible means so much to us.

It is the book of the covenant. It is the word, the conditions and the promises that marry us to the Lord.

We will look at the provisions. The first thing that strikes me about the book of the covenant is this: God is concerned with detail. The Ten Commandments are big commandments. They cover huge fields of human behaviour. But having given the Ten Commandments, God focuses in on detail and it is highly significant that we know the big rules but we are not so knowledgeable about the little ones.

What God is saying is that his will is to be done not just in the general principles of your life but in the particular details. He is concerned about your difficulties with your neighbours. Some of these things we would think were too small for God to be bothered with, but God is interested in everything.

I remember so clearly a dear lady called Grace Yunson who lived in the Shetland Islands in a little croft with a downstairs room and an upstairs room. There was no staircase but there was a ladder. Like many other women in that climate, she suffered dreadfully from rheumatism. One day a neighbour was in the house and Grace went to the ladder to go to bed. The neighbour went to help her up and Grace stopped at the bottom of the ladder, bowed her head and prayed. The neighbour said, "What are you doing?" She replied, "I'm asking the Lord to help me up the ladder." The neighbour said, "But I'm here to help you up." Grace said, "You're not always here to help me up and I always ask him." The neighbour said, "But you don't think God is interested in just that little detail of your life..." Grace responded, "If I can't trust him in the little things, I couldn't trust him in the big things."

In the same way, God, who knows how many hairs there are on your head, the God who even sees the sparrow hop to the ground, is concerned with detail. Not just the big Ten

Commandments, but the little details of the animals that you keep and how they behave.

The laws that he made divide up into two sections: what you might call the human relationships and the divine relationships. The first part of the book of the covenant concerns injuries to each other – between men and men and men and women. All the laws under that section begin with the word "if", as human laws do: *if* you do this then this must be done to you; because the laws are given for human beings, and the punishment in these cases must be given by human beings. This is God's rule for human relationships for criminal activity. If one human being hurts another then human beings have the responsibility to see that there is punishment. This is the principle of community in God's will and this is why there are law courts and this is why there are magistrates and judges. God wills this. It is our responsibility to punish human injury to another.

There are other crimes in God's sight, which are considered as being done to God. In these cases, the laws do not say "if you do this," the law says, "you shalt not do this" because if you do, God himself will punish in that case. He will not leave it to men. It is very interesting to see what crimes God considers are done against human beings and what he considers done against him, for which he will take personal responsibility.

Let us take the human injuries first from chapter 21 to 22:17. God is concerned with people, with slaves, with parents, with neighbours, with women. One of the remarkable things in this book of the covenant, when you compare it with any other law book of the ancient world is that God is concerned about more people. Under every other law code, a slave girl had no rights whatever. God says that a slave girl has rights and you cannot do anything with her that you wish. This was a revolution in the ancient world and God has a concern for women as well as slaves. Consider his concern for women here – the protection of pregnant women is something that is quite new in the ancient world. Wherever this book has gone, then human rights have followed; rights of every human being, even those considered without rights, and that is the thrill of reading the law of God. It is God who put these rights into human thinking. They were not there before for all human beings. The universal declaration of human rights by the United Nations could only be produced two thousand years after Christ came. It is an amazing document. I know that it was agreed by many other nations but it is a document that was only possible in a world where the Bible had been preached.

In this passage are the rights of women, slaves, parents and neighbours. The crimes that God is concerned about are also very interesting: assault, theft, murder. It is very interesting that murder and manslaughter are clearly distinguished. God has protection for those who have killed without malice or intention. That is one of the distinctions that English law has followed, thank God.

There are careful distinctions made here: rape, fraud, trespassing, borrowing without returning. I had better go and look at my bookshelves. Even more amazing: neglect. It even talks about a man who leaves the cover off his well because he cannot be bothered to cover it up after he has filled his bucket with water – and somebody falling in. God is as concerned about damage done to someone through neglect, something that you should have done and you just were not bothered to do.

Here is an amazing concern and it covers your neighbour's health, his property, his life, his faculties, his reputation and his animals. Some people are very surprised to learn what God says about slavery. Let me hasten to say first of all, that the slavery envisaged here is nothing like the dreadful slave trade between Africa and America which was one of the greatest blots there has ever been on the history of the human race. This is a bond service for six years. A man who could not meet his debts, who was financially insolvent, could give or sell himself into service for six years. He would be freed in the seventh year. It was one of the rules of this bond service among the Hebrews, a rule that you will not find elsewhere, that it was for a limited period and on the seventh year there was a year of freedom.

What is amazing is the provision for slaves voluntarily to stay on in the security of their masters. This was done by piercing the ear; the ear is regarded throughout the Bible as that part of the body, which symbolises obedience. It is interesting that the words "obey" and "hear" are the same word in the Hebrew language. "Hear the word of the Lord". "He that has ears to hear, let him hear" – and that means you listen and you are going to do what you are told. So his ear was bored to give a sign that he was voluntarily staying on with his owner.

I read a lovely prayer: "Lord bore my ear with your awl and fasten it to the cross." What a prayer. If you understand what I have been teaching, that prayer becomes a very beautiful prayer. "I want to be bound to your service".

So much for the human injuries. I make two points now, Man must do (1) the retribution – the principle of punishment and of justice to the criminal by the community. God says you must do this. Even capital punishment, which is here (which therefore clearly cannot possibly be a contradiction of "Thou shalt not kill", which God has just said) is to be done by the community. We have here an amazing law which was much later to be at the heart of the Greek and Roman laws but which is now called the *Lex Talionis*, the Law of Retaliation, which says, "an eye for an eye and a tooth for a tooth", and so on. I want you to know that that is an amazing just law.

It is a law designed to limit the punishment to that which is deserved. It is saying unlimited retaliation and revenge is wrong. But a person ought to suffer in proportion to the suffering they have caused. I want you to notice that that *Lex Talionis* is not applied to every crime. It is only applied here to the injury of a pregnant woman. It is applied twice elsewhere to equally serious crimes. In other crimes, the punishment is a fine in money of equivalent compensation. But here God is making it known that he regards very seriously indeed the case of an attack on a pregnant woman.

The punishment must go up to an equivalent of the injury and not beyond. It lets you see what God thinks of a woman who is not in a position to defend herself and should be thought of tenderly and carefully; this lets you see into God's mind.

The second thing is the principle of repayment to man. Amazingly, we have only just caught up with this in English law. God right at the beginning was showing that the best way to deal with a thief is to make him pay for what he has stolen. We are just beginning to think that is a good idea, but God said it all along the line that a person who takes from others should repay and in some cases because of the seriousness of what is done, really repay. You notice the principles of justice here. Words for the judge, for the plaintiff, for the witnesses: no bribes. I want you to notice that God said you must never take the side of the poor because he's poor. I have sat through cases in law courts and I have heard comments by people in the public gallery that because a man was high up the social scale he got off and because he was a professional he got his case dismissed or a very light dealing with, whereas "we poor people get the lot". I have also heard comments when someone did not even stop to consider whether a poor man was guilty or innocent but said he was poor. Now these are just comments – thank goodness they do not come from the bench. I have only heard them among the public as I have sat through various cases. Justice must not regard a man's social station or his bank balance. There must be no regard whatever to his position. Justice must be scrupulously fair. Witnesses and the judge must be absolutely above corruption and bribery. I have lived in an overseas country where the bribery that went on in the law courts made me thankful that I never came under the law in that country. I thank God that as of today I believe that our law courts are free from bribery. I pray that that may continue, and that before God our justice may be impartial.

Now the second part of the laws here are the things that God considers as being done to *him*. The interesting thing is that most of them are done to a person. God is saying that there are certain things done to people that you must punish and you will deal with; there are certain things done to people that I will deal with, because they are sins against me. If you remember that the human injuries were against slaves, parents, neighbours and women; God is now revealing that the injuries that are done to him are done to widows, orphans, strangers and the poor. Those who do not have anyone to stand up for themselves, he stands up for. Those who need someone to look after them, he is their guardian. What you do to them you do to him: widows and orphans. They have lost their men and they do not have a man to stand up for them now, to protect them. It is a wonderful thread of teaching that goes right through the Psalms: that God is a father to the fatherless. The cause of the widow is very near to the heart of God. What we do to the helpless, we do to him, and we must reckon with him. It is an amazing conception.

You notice that in this case he does not say it is direct injury to them. It is not what you do to them it is what you withhold from them that he counts us as guilty for doing; not so much destroying them or hurting them but just simply withholding from them what they need. Now here is an amazing picture of God. It is for this reason that James said that pure religion and undefiled before the heavenly Father is to "visit the widows and orphans in their affliction and to keep yourself unspotted from the world".

To help the needy is as important to true religion as holiness, according to the letter of James. God therefore is the judge of the widow and the father of the fatherless. What a lovely God, who notices when people don't have someone to care for them. He takes a special interest in them. Do you know the result of this is that, from the very beginning, the church has had a special concern for those who have not had anyone to look after them? You study the history of orphanages in our world and just see where the inspiration to look after unwanted children came from. It came from God. Indeed, in the days when the barbarians came into the city of Milan they went into the cathedral and got the bishop and said, "Show us where the treasures of the church are." He said, "They are kept in that room through that door." When the barbarians stormed through that door they found a room full of orphans being cared for by the church – the treasures of the church. This is what the church has done when it has been true to God's mind. God shows that it is him we have to reckon with if we neglect the needy. The retribution will come from him – he will notice, he will repay, he will hear, he will kill. In this case, he will deal with it personally.

Not only what people withhold from other people but what they withhold from God is in the book of the covenant – both treasure and time. Men must not withhold from God what he has a right to have. The first fruits of the harvest; one day in seven; one year in seven for your land; three religious pilgrimages a year, three feasts that he wanted them to come and give to him. In other words, God is teaching the Israelites that the principle of repayment is a very important one and he will hold people responsible for it.

We have had the book of the covenant, and in 23:20–33 we have the terms of the covenant given. There are two sides to this: what man must do, what God will do. First of all, take the human side. God reveals that there are three things he wants from his people: *submission*, *service* and *separation*. On our side, the covenant we have with our Lord is composed first of all of *submission*: not to rebel against our God, not to fight his word or his will, but to submit gladly and joyfully to everything he tells us.

Secondly, *service* – which includes worship. When they are told to serve the Lord their God here it is to worship and not just to work, it is both actually. To serve God includes your worship on Sunday and your work on Monday. That is why we talk about a meeting on Sunday morning as a service of worship. We serve God on Sunday and we serve God on Monday.

Thirdly, *separation* – we are to have nothing whatever to do with other religions. We must not even use the names of other gods in our homes. That is a strong law, but God knows that if you start playing about with other religions, if you start dabbling in other things, sooner or later the truth suffers. I have seen that happen so often.

One of the commonest barriers erected against the Word of God is when people say "What about all the other religions?" They have usually dabbled in a bit of Buddhism or read a bit of Islam, and so on. If you dabble in these things you are going to be at the point where you might get confused about which God you serve and which religion is true. On the divine side, God is showing that if you submit to him, if you serve, if you separate, then he will give you three things. First, he will fight your battles for you, get the victory and get you into blessing. He would get his people into the land. Secondly, he will enlarge your borders. The borders listed here Israel has never had. The ground that Israel has by title deeds from God, they have never had. In the time of Solomon they had about a third of it, but it stretches a way up to the borders of the Euphrates River, and they have never been that far up. I believe that when God says these are your boundaries he means it. Therefore the Middle East is going to be troubled from now on – indeed, I believe, till the end of history, till Christ comes back to be their king. The Middle East is God's barometer and what happens there reflects the events of world history and the ticking of the clock towards the midnight hour.

He would give them boundaries if they kept their side. Why have Israel not had their land yet in three thousand, five hundred years of history? I will tell you why: they have never yet kept their side of the covenant. They have never yet submitted wholly. They have never yet served wholly. They have never yet separated wholly – and the result is they have never yet had their boundaries where they should be. God's words mean: I'll give you all that I can but there is a covenant and if you are not submitting to me and serving me and separating from other gods, how can I give you all that I want you to have?

Not only boundaries, but also blessings are mentioned. Look at the blessings Yahweh wants to give: food; children, so that there would be no infertility or barrenness and no miscarriages; he wanted to give them physical health; he wanted to give them long life. But all these were dependent on their keeping the covenant. Finally, we come to what I have called the "probate" of this covenant. It is a Will and Testament and it needs to be proved; it needs to be sealed. When someone dies and leaves you some money, you cannot touch it until the thing has been to probate, until it has been settled and sealed properly. How then is this covenant sealed? Moses: come up, now go down again; come up again, go down again. The mountain is in the plain, Moses is going up and down as the mediator, and finally the day comes when if he is ready to take his promises, God will be married to him.

If two Bedouin sheiks met and mingled their blood, that could never be broken. It was the blood of a covenant. It is out of that background in the Middle East, that God himself brought this book. God says that the covenant seals with blood. So they brought animals, they erected a simple altar, simple stones, no steps to it to avoid wrong thoughts, no carving to it to avoid the cleverness of man intruding, just a few simple stones. They brought the sacrifice, they killed it, they caught the blood, and Moses took some blood and put it on the altar and then he took the rest and sprinkled the people. He said that the blood of these animals has sealed the covenant. You have said you will do all these things. God says he will bless you; you are sealed. It was centuries later – perhaps a thousand and a half years later – that Jesus took a cup and said, "This is my blood of the new covenant".

They put up twelve stone pillars to represent the twelve tribes. The blood was sprinkled on the people and they saw God, or at least they saw the pavement under his feet. That was wonderful enough. What is wonderful about a pavement? Do you ever look at pavements? No, but if you saw God's pavements you would. Don't laugh at the Bible's descriptions of pearly gates and golden streets and glassy seas and sapphires and jasper and onyx—this is how it is going to be. They saw the pavement made of sapphires. Fancy making a pavement of sapphires. That is what God is like – so rich, so glorious – and they saw the deep blue of a pavement beneath God's feet. Then Moses went up the mountain and God had written in stone. When Moses went up there were two blocks of stone and etched and graved into those stone were Hebrew characters, and God had written it all down. It was so important that God fixed the writing. Nobody must ever change this. Moses took it down and they all saw the mountain burning.

God makes it clear that the details of your life are all related to a covenant with his glory. There is the mountain top and the valley bottom. You can see the sapphire pavement, you can see his glory, but you have got to work it all out with your neighbour and with your animals and in your daily life and in your relationships and in your property and with other people's property. The glory of the Lord will somehow be related to all that and be made manifest in it. This is what is called working out your own salvation, for it is God who works in you.

From all this, two facts emerge. First: God is a God of absolute justice. Never listen to anybody who is trying to tell you that God is unfair. Every time you talk about the gospel, you will find somebody brings up a question which implies that God is unfair. I heard it at a college of law: "It's not fair of God to do this, and it's not fair of God to do that, and what about those who've never heard?" One can just say: From the Bible we know that God is just, absolutely just; I am not worried about the things that worry others, I know God well enough to know that whatever he does in the last day will be absolutely fair.

The other fact that emerges is this: God is not only justice, he is mercy. He provides an altar and burnt offerings and peace offerings. Why were those needed? Because God knew they would break his laws. God in his mercy has provided a way. It is the way of blood to offer a peace offering and a burnt offering and, later, sin offerings, so that those who broke his laws might find forgiveness, and that is why the cross had to happen. The commandments without the cross would damn us all to hell, but the cross will bring us to heaven.

READ EXODUS 25–27

We have seen that Yahweh, the God who made everything there is, was getting married to the people of Israel. A vow and a covenant was made between him and them which married them to him. They are his people forever and God never repents of that kind of promise.

Now what follows a marriage? Setting up house, furniture, decorations –that is the next thing. Therefore, it is quite normal and understandable that the very next chapters in the Bible after Yahweh and Israel have got married is to set up house together and to discuss furniture, colours, decorations and all kind of things. For the simplest meaning behind the tabernacle is that God was going to live with his people. They were now married and he was going to live with them permanently.

Of course, it had to be a temporary building because his people were going to move and therefore it needed to be a moveable house for God so that he could go on living with the people he had married. Into the modern period you can still go into the Arabian Desert and see a Bedouin encampment and find in the centre a large tent and you know that is the sheik's tent. Around the large tent are a lot of smaller tents, which you know are his brides'. This tabernacle is the sheik's tent. This tabernacle is where God was going to dwell, and wherever they stopped, around this big tent would be the smaller tents of his bride. It is a well-known pattern and God is simply fitting in to human patterns of arranging how to live.

Now this tabernacle is of God's design. No man ever decided a single detail of what you see there. God was the architect and he gave every last, little detail to Moses except, as far as we can see, the laver. Do you realise that you are looking at God's architecture? It tells us quite a lot about God, for an architect is an artist and you can tell a lot about the person of the architect from the building he has designed.

Now what can we tell about God from this? Here are five things straightaway. First of all, God has an eye for detail. It is not just the big thing, the shape of it all, but the hooks that join the curtains together. God is a God of detail. He takes as much care over the little things as the big things. He did not take more care over an elephant than over a fly.

A second thing that this tells me about God is that he is very straightforward. There is nothing complicated about this tabernacle, it is straightforward – square. You can understand it very simply. It is not a complex building when one looks at some of the structures architects are managing to produce today – there is a lovely simplicity about it.

Thirdly it tells me that God is very orderly. There is a mathematics about this. The holy place is a square; the holy of holies is an oblong, twice the square. There is something very fitting; it is not out of proportion.

A fourth thing that I gather from this is that God is more interested in quality than quantity. It is not a big place. It is not a huge, impressive palace, but it has got quality. It would have cost twice as much as a new church in Britain might cost, yet it is smaller.

A fifth thing that this tells me is that God is interested in colour and beauty. All the embroidery and the decoration is good and it is colourful. But these are just minor things compared with what this is meant to say. This tabernacle is meant to say far more than that. That could have been said in a few verses in the Bible and finished with. But it has been suggested that some fifty chapters in the Bible mention the tabernacle directly or indirectly, and the details of it. There is something terribly important here. God dismisses the creation of the world, in a sense, in a couple of pages in the Bible, and yet here we are told of every detail of the tabernacle. Do you think God wastes words? Why do you think God wrote all this out? Why does he want you to study this? Because he put it in your Bible, and he said "search the scriptures". Jesus told us to search the scriptures for they are about him.

One of the things that we're going to see is that as you look at that tabernacle you are looking at the Lord Jesus Christ. You are looking at a parable – a prophecy in material and gold and silver. Here is a prophecy that tells you what it is all about and it is pointing straight to Jesus. Now there are two things this tabernacle tells me basically about God that are extremely important. Number one: how *near* God is to his people; and, number two, how *far* God is from his people. The tabernacle, in an amazing way, brings God very near and yet puts him far away. It is this tension that is resolved in Christ. You see, we want God as near as possible. We want him to live with us, to be with us, to help us. We want him to share every day and yet we know that there is something in God we do not want to come near. We know that he may be physically near to us, but morally he is a long way from us.

This tension is the kind of uneasy relationship we have with God until we know Jesus. Before you know Jesus you want to say, "God, do I want to get near to him or do I want to keep away from him? Will he punish me because of my sins or love me in spite of them?" You want him to love you and yet the nearer you come to God, the more you feel that you are a sinner and he cannot come near to you, and there is this tension. The tabernacle resolved the tension for the Jews as Christ resolves the tension for the Christian. That is the pattern that we are going to look at now, a pattern shown to Moses up on top of the mountain.

Let us take the first lesson: the tabernacle tells us how near God is to his people. Think of it, God wants to live right where people live. He wants a tent right among their tents. Now this may seem a bit ludicrous to you, but to try and get the feeling; supposing you saw three or four doors away from your house a "For Sale" notice and you saw the people move out and you wonder who you are going to get as neighbour, and somebody says: "God is moving into that house. The curtains will always be kept drawn in that house so that you don't see God. You will see a column of smoke coming up from the roof of that house all the time when God is in residence; his standard as it were." Now how would you feel as you walked down the road? Would you cross the road to the other side to keep away from the house or would you go up to try and peek through the windows around the curtains? What would you feel if God was living just three or four doors down your street? That is how the Jews felt when they built this tabernacle. Before that, God was away up on the mountaintop and higher. The God who made the heavens and the earth, the God who made the stars, the nearest they got to him was as they were at the bottom of the mountain; he was four thousand feet up. Now he says that he is going to live in a tent right next to them. The cloud was going to come down and settle on the tent when God was in residence. Do you get a funny feeling about that?

They just had to look a few yards across the sand and there was God in his tent. There were curtains up all the time to stop you looking in. It must have given them a feeling of awe and reverence, but how amazing that God wanted to live a few yards away from his people; that he wanted to come right down to earth as it were. You see, this thread goes right through the Bible from beginning to end. "The tabernacle of God is with men and he will dwell among them and they will be his people and he will be their God." I am quoting now from the book of Revelation in the New Testament. This is like a golden thread running right through Scripture. God wants to live among people. He wants to come right down to the level of earth, and pitch his tent and tabernacle among us.

There is however one huge difference between the Old Testament and the New and it is this: in the Old Testament God dwells in *places*; in the New Testament God dwells in *people*. In the Old Testament God dwells in buildings – the tabernacle and later the temple; in the New Testament God dwells in believers. The tabernacle of God is no longer a building. It is no longer a temple. God does not live in a building any more.

Why the change? Well let me quote literally from the Greek language of John's Gospel chapter 1, "And the Word became flesh and tabernacled among us. We beheld his glory, glory as of the only begotten Son of the Father." That is what made the change. Up till the moment of Jesus coming, if God was going to dwell on earth he had to have a building. No person was adequate to contain God and so he had a building constructed.

First the tabernacle, when they were on the move, then the temple when they settled down in the Holy Land, but when Jesus came the temple was rendered obsolete. Frequently he visited the temple, but once while he was teaching in the temple he said: "Destroy this temple and I will build it again in three days," and they laughed at him. They said that the temple had been years in the building. Could Jesus build it in three days? John adds this word: "This he spoke concerning his body." The tabernacle of God was now the body of Jesus. God was among his people, living with them in the body of Jesus. But Jesus has gone back to heaven – where is the tabernacle now? Oh, we could build a temple or a cathedral or a chapel, but you cannot make a house of God with bricks. We ought never to refer to a brick building as a house of God. It never is, not now. Where is God's tabernacle now?

Well to bring it across I say this very bold thing to a congregation: "You're looking at it now and I'm looking at it now."

Know ye not, that you are the temple of God, of the Holy Ghost? Now God is still living with people. He is still down at the level of earth but now he is using people. He is dwelling in the temple of the bodies of believers. Isn't that an amazing thought? So that is why, in the New Jerusalem, the city of God whose builder and maker, architect, designer is God, when it comes down from heaven to replace all the cities that men and town planners have made, there will be no temple in that city. There will be no religious buildings in heaven at all – no churches, no chapels – but God will be in the midst of them. God will dwell among them and the word again is "tabernacle" among them because he will be there among them all and in them all.

Now that is the thread we are going to trace and this was the first tabernacle of God on earth. We are going to trace it right through and see in these curtains, in those boards, in that furniture, a picture of Christ and of Christians. For it is the same God in the Old Testament and the New Testament, and the places he lives in have the same characteristics as the people he lives in. If you are a believer, you are one of those boards. We are looking at Christ covering believers.

What I am saying here is not new. As you think about this, I want you to get the message. The Epistle to the Hebrews is the one letter in the New Testament you should read after you have read about the tabernacle. It talks there of the things in the Old Testament being "shadows" of things to come. Now what is a shadow? A shadow has no reality in itself; it is only there to take the shape of an object that is causing the shadow. It is as if here is Christ standing in the New Testament and his shadow falls back into the Old Testament and you can trace the shape of Jesus' shadow in this. You can see what he is going to be like by looking at the shadow.

Of course we now have what the New Testament calls the "substance." "The shadows of the Old Testament become the substance of Christ," says Paul in Colossians, and that is how we are going to approach it.

Now not only is God very near, not only has he come down to earth, "Emmanuel, God with us" when the tabernacle is put up and the Israelites are just outside, with the twelve tribes all around the edge and they must have felt God was terribly near them, yet the shape of this tabernacle showed that God was still a long way from you. You could not just walk from your tent to see God. There was a curtain there and you mustn't climb under it or over it. It's there to keep you out. You had to come in at the far end, far away from God. Ordinary people can only come in the first little bit, in the outer court.

The way is limited and there are veils hanging all the way in and you must not push past those veils—God dwells there. Only once a year could one man go in, and that was all. Keep away; keep out! In other words, the tabernacle was saying: God is very near, keep away. Why? The answer is to be found, as we will see, in the furniture that you have to pass all the way in. If you are ever going to get near to God, there are certain things that are going to be necessary. You are going to have to come through a door. You are going to have to visit an altar. You are going to have to wash. All the way in it is telling you that God is very near but you can't just walk into his presence – there are certain things to do first.

I can say this: that this part of the tabernacle talks about

God's approach to man and the conditions of it, but the rest of it talks about man's approach to God and that is how we are going to meet. God has approached man by coming down to earth and tabernacling among us, but how will man approach God? It is all there and there is no difference whatever between the meaning of the tabernacle and the teaching of the New Testament in all this. It is a perfect picture of salvation.

Let me just run through some of the details that will help you to understand. I am not going to spoon feed you. I want you to dig for yourself and meditate on these chapters until the very meaning becomes so clear that Christ himself steps out of the pages. We notice, for example, the variety of material used. The metals for example: gold, silver, and bronze. Now bronze is not what we understand by bronze. They had not yet, by a long way, discovered how to make bronze, as we know it today. It was an alloy of copper and tin, mainly copper. So you must imagine the colour, in a sense, of copper. We know there were copper mines in the Sinai Peninsula. We know also that in Egypt they used a great deal of copper and tin alloy, and this was what they had brought with them from Egypt.

Now you notice that the metals get steadily more precious as you move in towards God, and that is right and proper. In the human area, the metals are largely copper and tin alloy. Even the sockets at the base of the pillars are cheaper metal. But as you move in towards God, the bronze begins to fade away and the silver increases and the gold increases until as you move right into God, you have got solid gold. Here we have even the metals graded as it were from the human to the divine. You have a progression of thought.

Indeed you can say that the bronze speaks of humanity and human affairs, the pure gold speaks of deity and God, and the silver speaks of the metal that is the link between the bronze and the gold. Silver is always in scripture the metal of ransom, the metal of redemption. The silver shekel was what the Israelite used to redeem his first-born son. Our Lord was sold for thirty pieces of silver. It is the slave money price and the freedom money price. We shall see a deep significance of that when we come to the boards, but you can see the bronze of human workmanship, the pure gold of God, and the silver that is the link. Are you beginning to see the meaning of the metals?

Now there are colours here. Let me tell you the meaning of some of them. First of all, let us take blue. That requires little explanation – the blue of the heavenly colour. Blue has consistently been associated with that infinite space above us. Blue speaks of a sky; blue speaks of that which is above us, and this is one reason why many churches have often used blue. Scarlet has always been the colour of royalty. There are scarlet robes, and this is, as it were, the highest that man can get: the scarlet robes of royalty. On great State occasions you study the robes and see how much scarlet is used.

Now if you take the blue and the scarlet and put them together, what are you going to get? Purple – which has always been the in-between colour. There were many kings in the ancient world and they always wore scarlet. The gods inhabited the blue sky but the king of kings and the lord of lords (the title given to the Roman emperor), was in imperial purple colour. The emperor alone wore purple, as someone in between – above the kings of the earth, below the heavenly blue. That was where purple fitted in. It was considered as someone who combined the divinity of the blue and the royalty of the scarlet.

Here we have a perfect picture of the King of kings coming through. Someone who is a king on earth – yes he was king of the Jews – and yet someone who combines the heavenly. They called the Roman emperor "lord", but they also said

"Jesus is Lord," and the Christians refused to call anyone else king of kings and lord of lords. The materials used are interesting. Fine white linen is always used in the Bible of righteousness, as a bride wears white at her wedding. It is the same meaning: purity; chastity. So you get fine white linen around the circumference used here too. A basis of righteousness – God is clean; God is holy. There could only be one colour for the outer curtains around the court – fine white linens. In Revelation 19:8 we read that "the fine linen is the righteous acts of the saints". That curtain alone, without anything in the middle, would have been a reminder to the people that God is a holy God and requires righteousness.

The goat's hair that is used is associated many times in the Bible with prophecy and prophets. Elijah wore this; it is mentioned in Zechariah. Rams' skins dyed red—need I tell you what that speaks of? It speaks of lambs that have died, stained with blood, and it covered all of this. Rams' skins dyed red – a ram that had died, and the blood on its coat. Now the Authorized Version renders as "Badger skins" but there are no badgers in the Sinai Peninsula area. It was a Hebrew word that translators of the Authorized Version did not understand. It seems fairly clear that it was a goatskin covering.

If you saw the tabernacle from outside it would look terribly dull and uninteresting, wouldn't it? You would have no idea what colours there were inside, no idea what lay underneath. You would just say, "Oh well, it's an ordinary tent for that's the colour of every Bedouin tent" – a dark goatskin tent. You can see them in the desert, like black dots in the distance. That might be all you could see.

You know, that is all some people can see in Christ. They can only see a man – that is all. They don't see his death for them as a ram. They don't see any of his royalty and his deity. It is as if God is saying to them: "He hath no form nor comeliness that we should desire him when we see him." It is not human attraction. You will need faith to believe what is underneath, in Jesus, before you discover the deity and the beauty and the royalty and his atoning death for you. Do you see how it speaks of a very ordinary outside and all that richness buried under there?

The measurements of the tabernacle also seem full of significance. They are so carefully worked out, and numbers in the Bible are important. Here are just some of them and you can work out for yourself where we go from there.

The number three is usually associated with testimony. Three witnesses were considered adequate to establish truth. You will find a number of threes – three articles in the holy place, for example. You will find a number three giving a three-fold testimony. You see three areas: the court, the holy place, and the holy of holies. There are a number of threes here that are giving you a true testimony, each backing the others up.

Four is a figure that means universal, covering everything. We talk about the four winds and the four corners of the earth and the four points of the compass and there are certain things that have four points. The altars always have four horns to cover every direction that people may come to it.

Five is usually the figure of human responsibility, things that human beings need to do. The Ten Commandments are made up of two fives. Fives were things you learned on your finger as a child. God speaks to men about their responsibility in fives, perhaps so that we could remember them easily.

Seven is the perfect number in scripture. Six is therefore used again and again in scripture for human failure, human falling short of divine perfection, getting so far but falling short. It is no accident that the number of the beast in Revelation is 666. Trying to be God but falling short at every point.

Twelve is usually God's number for administering his affairs – twelve tribes, twelve disciples, and twelve gems on the breastplate signifying the twelve tribes. In the book of Revelation in chapter 21, the figure twelve is used nine times to describe the Holy City of Jerusalem. It is God's figure of arranging things: a dozen.

Finally, the figure forty is usually, in the Bible, a figure of testing or probation. Forty days and forty nights: forty years in the wilderness; our Lord also was forty days in the wilderness; there were forty days between the resurrection and the ascension. Forty days keep coming in as a period that God chooses to get a lesson across, to teach something.

We have got the substance and we can see the shape of the shadow so much more clearly.

READ EXODUS 28–31

When Christians read and study the Old Testament, there are two extreme reactions to avoid. One is too much influence and the other is too much ignorance. To put it another way, some Christians read the Old Testament as if the New Testament had not yet been written, other Christians read the New Testament as if the Old Testament had never been written. That sounds like riddles, but let me give you examples.

We have been looking at the tabernacle. We are now going to look at the priesthood, sacrifices and the Sabbath. As we do so, one of the dangers for Christians is to be too much influenced by these things – ordering their church life as if they were living back in the Old Testament days; starting to talk of a building as the "house of God", talk about holy furniture and the holy table, talking about their minister as a priest, talking about Holy Communion as a sacrifice and getting the Sabbath and Sunday confused. They have become too much influenced by the Old Testament and they have gone back into the old Jewish ways of thinking.

On the other hand there are Christians who have so dismissed all this teaching that they forget that God does need a holy building on earth. They forget that God does need priests on earth. They forget that blood is needed all the time in the Christian life – the blood of sacrifice. They get confused between Sabbath and Sunday and start applying Sabbath rules to Sunday and talking as if Christians are under the Sabbath law. Let us try to steer the right course between these two. We are going to look now at the priesthood: Aaron the high priest, and his four sons, the other first four priests. As we do so, let us never even say that a Christian minister is a priest. But let us remember that we still need a high priest and we have one, and we still need priests on earth and believers are a royal priesthood. This is the right kind of balance.

The New Testament does not abolish the Old; it fulfils it. That is why a Christian who does not study the Old Testament will not have a real grasp of the New. If there is one book I would love you to read after finishing Exodus, it is the Letter to the Hebrews – a Christian book. Unless you have read Exodus and Leviticus, you won't understand Hebrews. We look first at chapters 28–30, the consecration of the priesthood. God is letting Moses know that he would need mediators between sinful people and a holy God. For example, if I wanted to see the Queen and go and talk to her in Buckingham Palace it would be out of the question. I could go and I could stand at those iron gates and say to the sentry, "Look I want to see the Queen. I need to see her badly. She's the only person who can help me." That sentry has the duty to say, "I'm sorry, you cannot approach. You're a commoner, you have no right of access to Her Majesty; you stay right there."

If on the other hand I could get hold of a member of the Privy Council and say, "I wonder if you could go to the Queen and ask her on my behalf to sort this question out because she is the only one who can do this," and supposing he says, "Yes I'll go" – then I am in. My request goes right through to the Queen herself. Now that is a very simple illustration but do you realise that you have no right whatever to bring a single prayer to God *except* through Jesus. The world assumes that it has a right to pray, and therefore as soon as the world is in a jam then a prayer goes up: "O God help me", so whenever we pray it is through Jesus Christ our Lord. We cannot come to God without a priest.

Now let us look at Aaron and his four sons and see how their very dress speaks to us of Jesus. Why did they go to all this business of dressing up in a girdle and a robe and an ephod and a breastplate and shoulder plates and a turban and a gold plate here? I will tell you: because they were not Jesus; because Aaron was a human being and he lacked the qualifications needed. So to make up for his personal inadequacy he was dressed in those things, which represented adequacy for priesthood. Therefore when the High Priest comes who is adequate – no more robes; they are no longer needed. Aaron himself lacked those essential qualities, which were necessary for an adequate high priest. So God told Moses to make these garments so that when people look at him they do not see Aaron, they see the garments and they realise what a high priest is for.

Supposing I just went through these garments and various things that he had to put on in the order in which he put them on – that might help us. First of all he would put on a coat of fine linen – rather like to us a dressing gown, just a long coat with sleeves of fine white linen which we know already from the tabernacle curtains is a symbol of righteousness; the bride who wears white, purity. The second thing he would put on would be a robe around that – rather like a schoolmaster's robe – of heavenly blue. A heavenly priest is needed – not just a righteousness but a heavenly one. So he would put on a blue robe, beginning to look rather marvellous already. The third thing he would put on would be the ephod. Now this was a long strip of cloth with a hole right in the middle and the head goes through the hole and the cloth hangs down back and front. It is gorgeously embroidered in blue, purple and scarlet, and even gold thread woven in – the same colours as the curtains and the veil. It is back and front, hanging down. The reason for this is that the priest will go in and out on behalf of the people. He will go in to pray to God; he will come out to tell the people what God has said. Either way he is travelling and they will see the same colours as the veil, the curtain. It is almost as if part of the curtain is coming out to meet them. You can see the meaning. The fourth thing that he would put on would be the girdle. This was a kind of belt, a strip of material knotted and hanging down to hold everything together so that it didn't flap or blow about, remembering that he would walk through the open air courtyard, but a girdle is always a symbol of service. "He girded himself and washed their feet," it says of Jesus. To gird yourself is to say, "I am at your service, I am a minister; I am here to serve; a servant."

The next thing he would put on would be the breastpiece. This was a nine-inch square gold plate, double skinned with a hollow in between, and on the front plate of gold there were twelve stones set in. Each was engraved with the name of one of the twelve tribes of Israel. We are told that this had to hang down so that it lay on his heart. When the priest went in, his heart held his people in compassion and love. When he went in to pray, the people were there resting on his affections – it is a lovely symbol.

Within the hollow between the two plates, we are not told exactly but it looks as if there were two stones kept: black and white called the *urim* and the *thummim*. When a person was in a quandary, in perplexity about what they should do, they said to the high priest, "Will you go and pray to God and then will you come out to me and will you put your hand inside and pull out a stone? If it is the white stone, the answer is 'yes,' God wants me to do this; if it is the black stone the answer is 'no'." Now it is a crude and rather simple way and yet God honoured it.

EXODUS 28-31

In those days God guided the hand of the priest to bring out the right stone to give his guidance to his people. It is a symbol of the fact that if you want guidance you go to Jesus for it. We could have a book for our religion which told us every mortal thing to do, but we do not have that. There are many questions in your life that the Bible will not answer and it would be wrong to claim it does. You have to choose between two jobs—the Bible doesn't have a specific answer dealing with that situation. You will need further guidance. How do you get it? You go to your high priest and you say, "Is it yes or no?"

On the shoulders of the high priest there were more gold plates and the twelve tribes of Israel were engraved. He carried them not only on his heart but on his shoulders. The shoulder is the place of strength. The shoulder is the burden bearer. Not only to carry them on your heart in affection but on your shoulders for responsibility. We have a high priest who carries us on his shoulder as well as on his heart. I love to think of the story of the lost sheep here. Have you seen a shepherd carrying a lamb, or even a sheep, that is exhausted? Round the back of the neck, both legs down. I have done it myself. You carry the sheep along on your shoulders and you bring the sheep home. The priest carries the tribes of his people on his shoulders next to his heart.

Finally, on his forehead there was a gold plate hanging down from the turban and the turban was the last thing put on. It was more a mitre, a crown, a royal headpiece. Hanging from it by two chains was the gold plate: "Holiness to the Lord". We are told that he had to wear this in case any of the offerings were imperfect. In other words, the human machinery of offering could break down and the offering could be less than perfect, but because the priest is separated to the Lord, God accepts the offering for the sake of the priest. It is holy. I am very conscious and so are you that an act of worship is far from perfect. How we wish we could worship really perfectly and say that it is a perfect service. It never is. You will always be able to find something wrong with the service if you want to. If you come in a critical mood, you can always go home and talk about the preacher or the choir or that person who coughed all the time. You can always go home and grumble and you can always find fault with an offering of worship. Beware lest the devil gets you into a critical mood, as if you have come to church to judge the worship. You haven't, you have come to worship to be judged. If God were strictly just he would say at the end of the service, "That was not perfect. That was wrong. That could have been better done. The singing could have been better, and that hymn could have been arranged better." But God doesn't, he looks at our high priest and says: "That covers. My high priest, holy to the Lord, covers the imperfect offerings of his people."

Isn't all that meaningful? It is all in Jesus, so Jesus did not need to wear an ephod. He did not need to wear a breastplate. He did not need a black and a white stone. He did not need a turban. Jesus came as he was, the perfect high priest, and we have got all we need in him. That is why we don't dress up now. We don't need to because I know I am imperfect and I cannot cover those imperfections by dressing up in all kinds of marvellous gold robes. I am covered by a high priest and he takes the imperfect offering of my service and God accepts it, and he accepts your imperfect worship for the same reason. Praise God.

Now let us look at the four priests Nadab, Abihu, Eleazar, and Ithamar. Not only do the people of God need a high priest, they need priests. The glorious truth for us is that we are a priesthood. In those days, you notice, the priest had very simple clothing. Four things are mentioned, none of them terribly rich, none embroidered, none of them gold, but pay attention to the list. In the order of putting them on, again: number one, underclothes. That is interesting – it was not mentioned for the high priest but for the priests: linen white underclothes. They would never be seen, nobody would ever know whether they were worn or not, but God would see. God's priests are to start with the unseen things. "Cleanse thou me from secret faults," said the Psalmist. If I may put it this way: God looks at your spiritual underclothes. Do you understand? He doesn't look at the outward appearance, the Lord looks on the heart, and he wants you to be clothed right from the inside through to the outside. The second thing they had to put on were coats: white linen; girdles for service; bonnets or caps. In other words, his priests are simply to be good right through, and we are his priests today – all of fine linen, and the symbolism is there. To be concerned about Sunday clothes and not about the state of your heart is to live in the Old Testament and not to be in the New.

Now let us turn to the next stage: chapter 29. Now Christ is seen not in the high priest's robes but in the offerings. Once again, to those of us who have never been accustomed to sacrifice it is offensive to think of blood. You do not expect your minister to be there with a butcher's block and an axe or a knife, taking an animal, slitting its throat, catching its blood in a basin, and then sprinkling it on your clothes, the pews and the pulpit. Quite frankly, I think you would probably think the minister had lost his sanity if you found him doing that. The danger is that because you are not used to it you do not think about it. Indeed, the blood might offend to our modern susceptibility, our sensitivity, our fine taste. It was even on those beautiful robes that were made – they would have been sprinkled with blood. Some people don't like blood at all, some people faint at the sight of it, but there it is and it is very pleasant to God. Here we have to do a thorough rethink. What is unpleasant to us is pleasant to God and we have got to ask who is right. Some people are so offended and so put off by all the sacrifices of the Old Testament that they say, "I don't want even to think about it. I don't like these passages, I don't like the book of Leviticus, it is just a bloodbath, like an abattoir, not a tabernacle." But to God it was very pleasant. The burnt offering, the sin offering, the wave offering, the peace offering – all these sacrifices, God enjoyed them. May I say this? The first question we could ask on a Sunday morning is this: is God enjoying this service? Is it a pleasant service to God? It might be a service that is not very pleasant for us, but if God enjoys it, isn't that why we are there? It may be a service that puts us off in some way, but God says it is pleasant in his sight.

Why should God enjoy blood? I will tell you why: because he loves to forgive sin and until blood is shed he cannot do it. He loves to have fellowship with people, and until sin is dealt with, he cannot do it. When he sees the blood he says, "Now I can forgive them. Now I can have fellowship, now I can come to my people," and that is very pleasant to him. Now if it is true that we do not need sacrifices any more, let us not forget that this is only because the blood of Jesus goes on cleansing. At the heart of our Christian worship is an act of remembering blood—the wine. I want you to see blood when you look at it because that blood of Jesus is what stands between us and God and enables us to have fellowship with him – so we must not be put off by sacrifices. We must not go back to the Old Testament and start calling our table our altar and our minister a priest. But on the other hand we must not forget the blood.

This is reflected in hymns. Some decades ago there was a reaction to hymns about the blood, and they began to die out, gradually shrinking in number. Therefore, God may not enjoy the singing quite as much.

When Aaron and his priests were all dressed, they were

sprinkled with blood and all the way in the doorway, the altar, the laver, all the way in, everything blood, blood, blood – right through to the altar of prayer, the altar of incense. Even the prayer had to have the blood on it.

Notwithstanding that past change in traditional hymns, I find today that there has been a rediscovery among God's people of the power of the blood of Jesus and there are more choruses being written about the blood of Jesus once again. People are using the power of the blood and pleading the blood of Jesus in crises, and that is a wonderful sign. They are realising that if we are going to come to God, it is blood all the way. We may not need sacrifices today but that is only because the blood of Jesus speaks louder than the blood of Abel.

Incense was used – prayer. The little prayer altar is one of the loveliest pieces of furniture in the tabernacle. It would stand about the height of a pulpit, some eighteen inches square. Shall I tell you what that says to me? The altar of prayer, the altar of incense does not have much length, and not much breadth, but it has depth. I don't think that is a coincidence, do you? What kind of prayer does God like? It is the prayer that's deep. "Don't think that you will be heard," said Jesus, "for your long prayers". It is not the length of the prayer it is the depth. It was just a little human piece of furniture. Every morning and evening Aaron the priest would put a pinch of incense on and keep the prayer ascending to God. It is a lovely picture of a priest's duty and Christ ever lives to make intercession for us. The coals from the altar came from the burnt altar, from outside, and were carried in on a shovel. So that from the place of sacrifice came the fire of the prayer. Do you see all the meaning of it?

We could think of the washing with the water. They must never go in to pray unless they have washed first. Clean people can pray effectively. "The prayer of a righteous man is effectual in its workings," said James. So wash first, then pray. The oil of anointing, or the oil that ran down Aaron's beard – what does that symbolise? When her majesty Queen Elizabeth II came to the throne, a little vial of oil was used to anoint her. It was called in the service "the chrism". For the word "anoint" and "chrism" and "Christ" are the same word. "Christ" means anointed one. "Christian" means an anointed person. If you call yourself a Christian then you are calling yourself an anointed person, but anointed with what? Oil is throughout the Bible a symbol of the Holy Spirit and a Christian should be a Spirit-anointed person. As Christ our high priest was the anointed one, and as he stood praying after his baptism, the Holy Spirit descended on him, and by the power of the Spirit he went out to preach and to heal – the anointing. "Blessed is that oil that ran down Aaron's beard" – anointed of God for his task.

Finally, money was needed to keep the priests. Do you know how it was given? There was ransom money. Every adult person had to bring about half a shekel. It did not matter if you were rich or poor – half a shekel to them. Now it is interesting that it was the same for everybody. Do you know it costs the same for everybody to be saved? It does not matter if you are a millionaire or a beggar, it costs exactly the same to ransom you and set you free. That puts us all on an equal footing, doesn't it? There is no room whatever for distinction of wealth in the church.

James has some pretty strong things to say about giving a place to a rich man when he comes into your church, and telling a poor man, "Sit over there on the floor." No place for wealth because it costs exactly the same for every man, rich or poor, to come to God. Half a shekel – and it cost you not silver or gold but the blood of Jesus to come.

We come to chapter 31. There are two things said in this chapter—one about our work and one about our leisure. The key word is "work", which is not a very popular word. First of all, God has told them everything they need to know: the details of the tabernacle, the details of the priestly robes. Now they need to make it. He has called, he has filled and he has given; he has commanded. God not only tells you what to do, he tells you who is to do it, and he gives the ability to do it. We should never need to worry about the Lord's work. If he tells us to do a thing, he will supply the person to do it, and give them the gifts.

God chose Bezalel and Oholiab. Do you know what training those men had had for carving gold and wood and making embroidered curtains? I'll tell you. The training they had had was making bricks of clay. That is all the apprenticeship they had had. Isn't it marvellous? God took brickmakers and had given them the ability to fashion gold for him. It is not just your natural abilities God can use. He can give new abilities, which you never had before, and the tabernacle would be built by men who had got these abilities. How did they get them? I will tell you. Bezalel and Oholiab had a Pentecostal experience. They were filled with the Spirit of the Lord. The result was gifts in their hands that could do these things.

Finally and here I read something I found a deep challenge to my own heart and I think it will be to yours. God said: "While you're building the tabernacle, don't do any work on the Sabbath." Why not? Because it is terribly easy to be so busy doing God's work that you have no time for God. Do you understand the message? They could have said, "Oh, but it's the tabernacle. It's for God. It's his work and I'm sure he understands because it's his work." God was saying: no, you would die if you touch this job on the Sabbath even though it is my work; it is so important that you should rest in me, that even though you are doing my work, none on the Sabbath.

What is the Christian fulfilment of this? Don't let us

live in the Old Testament; don't let us go back to the Sabbath law. It is striking that in the New Testament the one commandment that is never mentioned for Christians is that fourth one, "Remember the Sabbath day". It is equally striking that when Paul went to the Gentiles who never did have a weekly day of rest, he never told them to keep the Sundays as a day of rest. To think that the Sabbath equals Sunday is to confuse the old symbol with the reality. What is the reality? Let me tell you, it is not Sunday observance. The reality is this: "There remains therefore a Sabbath rest for the people of God", and that Sabbath rest is to cease from your own works. If you want to read it all it is in Hebrews 4. It is a rest that the Jews did not get into even though they kept the Sabbath. You can keep Sunday observance and still not know the rest of the Lord. How do you enter into the rest of the Lord? In all your work for the Lord, enter into the fact that it is not your work at all, it is his. Cease from your own works. Jesus didn't tell you to build his church, he said, "I will build my church." He made the world and then stood back and rested. So with all your works: stand away from it; rest in God. Sabbath rest is not a rest you can have one day in the week, it is a rest seven days a week. It removes the striving and the struggling and therefore, since you are doing God's work and ceasing from your own, what you erect will last and be beautiful. It is his and it will go according to his plan. Otherwise, without entering into this rest you struggle and you strive to do it in the strength of the flesh, to do it with your natural abilities, and you get more and more overburdened with it all. Enter into his rest. There is a Sabbath rest for Christians and though it is expressed in our Sunday, it is not limited to that. It is found whenever a person ceases to try and do his own works and refreshes his soul in God's works.

READ EXODUS 32–34

No man has ever seen God, but many people have wanted
to. There is an echo in each of our hearts of Philip's words,
"Show us the Father and we will be satisfied." It is felt to
be one of the greatest handicaps of the Christian religion
that we worship an invisible God. People say, "If only you
could prove his existence, if only you could demonstrate
him to our senses, we would believe." Human nature says
that seeing is believing, but it is not. If you see, you do not
need to believe. It is because we find it much easier to take
in knowledge through the eye than the ear that we would
rather see God than hear him. But faith comes by hearing and
that is why God speaks to us in words rather than pictures.
Faith comes by hearing, and hearing by the word of God.

Faith is able to see the invisible; faith is able to hold the
intangible. One of the common temptations of the human
nature is to want an idol. Idolatry is almost the besetting sin
of human religion. We want a god we can touch, a god we can
see, a god we can point to, a god we can take other people
to and say, "There, look, that is the god who redeemed us."
We are reading in these chapters the account of the people
of God themselves who did not want to hear God but did
want to see him.

Remember that, just a few weeks before these events, God
has spoken to them directly; it sounded like thunder up in
the mountain top. They were so afraid they said, "Moses,

you go and talk to God. Don't let him talk to us, we don't like listening to God." But as soon as Moses went up the mountain, the people asked his brother, Aaron: give us a god we can see. They did not want to listen to God; they wanted to see him – they wanted a god for the eyes not a god for the ears, and this is the heart of idolatry.

Now make no mistake about it, they were not thinking of turning to another god other than Yahweh. They were not going to break the first commandment, "Thou shalt have no other gods before me," they were going to break the second, which was: "Don't make any graven images". They were not to try to make the invisible God visible. You cannot model God; you cannot draw a picture and say that is what God is like. You cannot produce a piece of sculpture in stone or wood. While Moses was up in the mountain talking about the tabernacle and the high priestly robes and all the beautiful things that were going to be made to help people understand God, they were down on the plain, making a "god". Bear in mind that all this time that Moses was up there, they neither had Moses nor the beautiful tabernacle, which yet had to be built. It was still all in God's mind, and now in Moses' mind, and Moses could see all the things that we have looked at: the tabernacle and the robes. But there was one striking omission from the tabernacle. There is something that is not in the tabernacle that you would find in every other religious building of those days and that is an idol. There is a house for God to be built, there is furniture for God, but there is no image of God in the tabernacle. It is the one thing that Israel, down on the plain, was making while God was telling Moses what kind of a house and furniture he wanted. They were not thinking of a house and furniture or robes, they were thinking of an image. So they got hold of Aaron and they pulled off all their earrings at his request. He says they were put in a fire and out came a calf. The

Bible more truly says he moulded it and he carved it and he produced a calf. Why a calf? Because that had been one of the most common idols in ancient Egypt. It was a figure of a young bull, signifying virility, and also indicating that many of the ancient religions came under the heading of what we call "fertility cults". But this calf was to represent God. They weren't calling it another god; they were calling it Yahweh. They were going to be able to point at it and say, "This is the god that brought you out of Egypt. You can see him now. You don't need to believe in an invisible god, he is a visible one."

There is another great advantage in having an idol: one is that you don't need faith any more – you can see. The other is that the idol is under your control, whereas God is not. Now let us just make that point a little more clearly. Prior to this, God appeared as a pillar of cloud and fire, and when that moved, they moved; when that pillar stayed, they stayed. They could not decide when to move – God decided when to move. But once you have got an idol you can say, "Come on, pick up the idol, we are going to take it off next Monday and we'll follow it along." You can control the idol — the idol can't tell you what to do. So man has been guilty of idolatry ever since the beginning as far as we can make out. An idol is visible and moveable, and you do the controlling. So the people of Israel sought an idol. Not only did Aaron give them a form of god to look at, he gave them a festival, and people love parties. If you want to have a popular religion, have plenty of idols and plenty of festivals and you are in. You will get a wonderful following straight away.

People love to worship through the senses and they love sensations. So forms and festivals are the two things that will make a religion popular. Aaron was saying: now we've got a calf, tomorrow we are going to have a celebration — a party; we will start in the morning with the religious side and after that, whoopee, we are going to have a great time. Of course, this was very popular. But one of the inevitable progressions downward for the human heart is this: if you worship with the senses, sooner or later you become too interested in the sensational, and the sensational will give way to the sensual.

You notice that all three words begin with the same sound, they are related words, and they are related things: senses, sensational, and sensual. That is precisely what happened under Aaron – they worshipped God with the senses. Through their eyes they wanted to see God. It became a sensational thing: a golden calf made out of their earrings, a dazzling piece of sculpture, something that was quite out of the ordinary. Then it became sensual and they had their wild party. You can imagine what it was like in those days: the senses, the sensational, the sensual. All this time Moses was up the mountain, planning the future, even planning the robes for Aaron, as the future high priest, and Aaron was down below doing this. Here is a picture, which I want to draw out. It may well be that God in heaven has a plan for our life and while he is planning it all out, and while he knows what he wants to do for us, we are doing something down here that is just not his will. What a contrast! Aaron had no idea at this stage what he was going to wear before the Lord. What he was doing was taking his clothes off at the foot of the mountain.

They had no idea that they were going to have a beautiful tabernacle for God to live in, with lovely furniture, and meaningful curtains. They had no idea, and they were building a golden calf. It was in this way that men and woman missed God's plan for them: they do what they think is best, they do what they enjoy, what they find helpful, and God in heaven is planning something quite different. How important it is for us to go into God's plan, not to do what we enjoy, not to do what we think helps religion, but to follow God's beautiful plan and to be in his will.

We turn now to chapter thirty-three. Basically, God said they were a stiff-necked, obstinate people. It took them six weeks to break the Ten Commandments – just six weeks since they said everything he said we will do. Six weeks later they have broken both tablets. There were five Commandments on one tablet, five on another, and in each they broke the second one. Breaking the second one in relationship to God made them break the second one in relationship to people; it follows as the night follows day.

Now God is very angry, so angry that he says to Moses: "Your people whom you brought out of Egypt, look at them; your people, you brought them out". Fancy God saying that, because they are now back at the human level – no longer God's people whom God brought out. They are now Moses' people whom Moses brought out; and God is ready to finish with them: Moses, you are the only one I can trust. I am going to start a new people of God with you – and it might have happened. The word "Israel" might have dropped out of existence at this point. There might have never been an Israel; there might have been a Moses people and Moses prayed.

His prayer is one of the most wonderful prayers you will read in the Bible. He says, "Lord they are your people and you brought them out of Egypt – not mine, yours." He appeals to: God's goodness in the past – his promises to Abraham, Isaac, and Jacob; God's grace in the present – to forgive; and God's glory in the future – what will people say if you let us down now? Now those are three tremendous appeals and every time you pray you can appeal to those three things and God will hear your prayer: God, I appeal to your promises in the past; your pardon in the present, and your glory in the future. It is your glory that is at stake. What a prayer – that is the way to pray; that is storming the gates of heaven. It is being very bold, but in holy boldness. God changed his mind. Think of the power of prayer to change God's mind. Did you ever realise you had that power when you got on your knees? Because God will – he loves a person to pray like this. He loves someone to claim his promises; he loves a man to challenge him to keep his glory. He changed his mind and he said, "Alright, I won't. But Moses, go down and deal with them," and Moses came down the mountain.

The interesting thing is that he had not seen all this until then. God was angry because God had seen it, and Moses pleaded with God. When Moses saw it he got more angry than God did. Did you notice that? Moses had pleaded for them tenderly, came down and when he saw it he smashed the tablets of stone. They were about eighteen inches by twelve inches, two of them; just lumps of granite and he threw them down. What a symbolic action, they had broken them anyway so he broke them too, and he said, "You've broken them," and then he destroyed the calf.

How to get rid of it? Gold is not an easy thing to dispose of. If he buried it, somebody is tempted to go and pick it up again. How could he get rid of it in a way that meant they could never touch it? He chose an extraordinary way. He chose a way that would leave that gold behind in their sewage when they left the camp. What a symbolic thing to do; he made them drink it so that they would not be tempted to go back for it. That got rid of the golden calf.

What else did he do? He got hold of Aaron and questioned him. Aaron shows up as a rather weak man; Aaron says, "Well you know how these people are." He was a man who was thinking not first of what God wanted but of what people wanted. He was playing to the gallery. He was a man who was concerned about what the people of God wanted, not what God wanted for his people. So he gave in and it came out. They wanted a bit of a do. They wanted somebody to look at, they wanted a celebration so he gave it to them.

"What about this calf," said Moses. Well, you know how it is when you put a bit of gold in a furnace you never know what is going to come out.... Isn't it feeble that a grown man can stand there and say, in effect, that it was just circumstances?

We have talked like that and said, "Well, I got into bad company and you know, life has been pretty pressured. You know what happens; you know what these people are like anyway."

Moses rebuked Aaron and stopped the orgy and he did it in a remarkable way. He stood at one end of the camp and he said, "Come on, you must decide whose side your are on. If you're on the side of Yahweh then come over here and do what the Lord tells you." One by one a group of people left the wild scene and came over to Moses. All his own relatives, all the tribe of Levi came – and Moses was of the tribe of Levi. They knew their own relative and they were on the Lord's side. He told them to deal with those who were still carrying on, clearly implying that they had refused to stop when Moses came, and three thousand people died that day.

What a contrast it was when the Spirit was given on the day of Pentecost – three thousand people lived. The law kills, the Spirit makes alive. But you go through the law to the Spirit; the law has to kill you dead before the Spirit can make you alive. The law has to take away your excuses and show you sin, then the Spirit comes and brings life, peace, joy and righteousness.

The most remarkable thing of all is that Moses was going back up the mountain. He was going to try to make atonement for their sin. Up to that point the atonement for sin was a lamb, a bull or a goat. But Moses knew that that would not do – it was not enough. So he went up the mountain and he said, "Lord, block me out of your book". God wouldn't let Moses do that. He would not let anyone do that, not until Jesus came.

But Moses tried to offer himself to God. What love he must have had for his people. Could you say honestly to God, "If you'll take all my relatives to heaven you can leave me out." (I don't think I could.) Paul said about his own people the Jews: "For I could wish that I myself were accursed and cut off from Christ for the sake of my brothers, my kinsmen according to the flesh."

Jesus did say it and do it. You can have me; save them. Moses tried so hard. God said that he would destroy them and make Moses everything, but Moses did not want to be saved if God was not going to save them. What an amazing prayer.

Just suppose that God had blotted Moses out of his book – can you imagine the Bible without Moses? No mention of Moses, no Law of Moses, nothing about Moses in this book – there would have been a great hole left. God did not blot Moses out of his book. But he said: you can go to the Promised Land but not with me; I will send an angel, a deputy. That was the next thing that Moses had to pray about in chapter 33. Wouldn't you be glad to have an angel to walk with you personally? I will tell you something better than an angel and that is to have God. Moses said to Yahweh: "Remember too that this nation is your own people. Yahweh replied: "I myself will go with you...." Once again, Moses had holy boldness and the Lord granted his request. It would be a good prayer for any church: God, we are not going unless you go with us. Your presence is what we need.

Up and down the mountain Moses goes. I was looking at a photograph of Mount Sinai and thought Moses must have been pretty fit. Though he was getting well on in years, he was over eighty, and he climbed up and down a four thousand foot mountain. No effort was too great for this old man to get the people right with God. He was not a man who retired from God's work. He went down again and he told the people. They stripped off their ornaments and they took off all their jewellery. Some of it had gone into the golden calf; the rest of it would be needed for the tabernacle. But it was not a time to adorn themselves; their lives were not now lives that could be adorned.

Do you know that for many a long year after that, the Jews did not wear any jewellery? They didn't adorn themselves. The tragedy is that centuries later they began to adorn themselves and they began to build golden calves again. By the time of Amos there were two golden calves at Bethel and Dan. They had all come back again. It is a constant danger this. Well they took off their jewellery and Moses, who had not yet built the tabernacle, took his own tent and put it outside the others, outside the camp, and he used to go and talk with God. That saved him going up the mountain in a sense. He used to go and talk there face to face, and God said, "Moses, you are my friend." I can't think of anything that I would rather be called by God than that, can you?

Abraham was called the friend of God, and Jesus said, "You are my friends if you do what I have commanded you" and, "I have called you friends". Moses talked with God as a friend.

So Moses, having got so friendly with God, said to him, "God I'd like to see your glory." Now here is an amazing thing: the Israelites said to Aaron, "We want to see God," and Aaron tried to make them a God they could see. Moses said, "I want to see you God," but he didn't try to make something to see. God said, "Well, if I let you see all of me it would be too much for you; I'll let you see just a little bit."

It is the mercy of God that we have to worship an invisible God. If God were visible you would be blinded and worse, it could even mean that you would be exterminated. No man has seen God, no man could and live; we are not fit to do so. That is why God in his mercy says: no you don't see me, you believe in me without seeing. Like Moses you can see a little bit of his glory. Moses get into this bit of rock, get right in. I will cover you up until I am right past and then you can just see the trailing clouds of glory; just a little bit that I leave behind.

Do you know, that is what you see now? That is what we see of God now, we see what he leaves behind when he has passed that way. You see the results of the touch of his Spirit in the life that has been changed. You see he has been by; something has happened and you see just a bit of his glory reflected. That is what Moses saw that day.

Moses wanted something else: to know what the name of Yahweh meant. Here are five things that God reveals his name means. I have transliterated them in English, or translated them into an alternative five words you can remember. They are five "P"s: pity, patience, purity, pardon and punishment. He pities us. He is full of pity – thank God he is. He's patient, slow to anger and long-suffering. When he is angry it is after he has been mightily provoked. He is a God of purity, holiness, righteousness. He is a God of pardon – he forgives thousands their iniquities. He is a God of punishment – if you play the fool you will ruin a generation but the effect will go on down for three of four more.

Moses asks God: are you going to go with us? God says he will renew the covenant. He will conquer their enemies. That is my side of it and on their side, they are to keep his commandments. Moses was to get two more bits of stone and the commandments would be written down again. The festivals they were to keep were: unleavened bread, redeeming your firstborn, the Sabbath rest, the feast of Pentecost, the feast of ingathering. It was the ones Yahweh gave that they were to keep; not their own festivals.

Of course we are Christians and we are not bound by any one of the festivals of the Jews. We are to keep the festivals in a new way; we are to keep the festival of unleavened bread by putting away malice. We are to keep the festival of redeeming the firstborn by dedicating our best to the Lord. We are to keep the festival of the Sabbath rest by ceasing from our own works and resting in his. We are to keep the feast of Pentecost or harvest festival by being filled with the Spirit. We are to keep the feast of ingathering by gathering all who will come, and look forward to the feast of the ingathering at the second coming of Christ. But we are to keep the festivals in a Christian way.

The last thing I have to say about this is the most exciting to me: Moses came down from the mountain and he did not realise that people would see God in his face. They wanted to see God; they had wanted to see what God is like and so they made a golden calf. But when Moses came down from the mountain, he had a golden face; it shone like gold and they looked at it and they could see what God was like. His face was luminous, radiant with God's glory; he had been talking to God. That is what people should see when we go out after a service of worship. They should see as we come out the door what God looks like.

God wants people to see himself, but not in a graven image. There is in our place of worship no ornament, no decoration, no jewels, no graven images; it is just simple, straightforward. But I hope people will see God in that place and see the glory. How will they do it? They will see the glory of God when they see people who have been talking with God – who don't realise that when you have been talking to God it shows.

Moses hung a veil on his face and did not want them to see that it would fade. But says the New Testament, "We all" (all of us now, not just one in the people of God, not just Moses) "reflecting as in a mirror with unveiled face the glory of God, are being transformed into the same glory day by day." Oh yes, people want to see God. So they make their idols and images and they dress objects up and they fail. But God wants to be seen in the people of God.

The Father was seen in the face of Jesus Christ and we beheld his glory, glory as of the only begotten son of the Father, full of grace and truth. For the Law came by Moses, but grace and truth came by Jesus Christ and there was glory. The face of Christ is to be reflected in our faces and in the people of God, that people may see his glory and know that he has passed by, and see the glory that lies behind. That is how we shall see God, until one day we no longer see through a mirror darkly, but face to face.

READ EXODUS 35–40

My ministry in a local church in Guildford saw the construction of a new building, the Millmead Centre, and I happened to be teaching on Exodus at that time. Studying the tabernacle, you will understand that in my mind I was comparing and contrasting the new place we were building with that tabernacle described in Exodus. How very different! The most obvious difference is that the tabernacle in Exodus was a portable building that could be pulled up, carried and set up somewhere else. I don't think anybody would manage to do that with the Millmead Centre – they really would have a job! Another difference lay in the things that are not in the tabernacle that were in ours.

For example, there were no windows at all in the tabernacle whereas we have glass everywhere. There are no seats in the tabernacle for the people but we spent quite a lot of time designing some comfortable pews. There was no pulpit in the tabernacle and no provision for musical instruments. But the biggest and deepest difference is this, and I hope I won't startle you too much by saying this, but the tabernacle was built for God whereas our new centre was being built for people. That is why the decoration and design were so different. I dread to think what the bill would have been for our building if we had coated all the reinforced concrete with gold leaf. Or if, instead of lead and aluminium on the roof we had used silver and bronze. I just dare not think of the bill, but then, we are doing it for people; the new tabernacle was perfectly designed for God. To underline this difference, there were rooms in the tabernacle into which people could not go; they were for God. But there is not a single place in our new centre where no-one could go.

Now we are going to look at the furniture, decorations and construction of the tabernacle and see why God wanted it this way. What was he telling us? We begin with the innermost room because that is where God starts, and we are going to start with the furniture. That is an interesting thing in itself. We tend to start with a building, and having got the building we say, "Now, what sort of furniture will fit into this?" and we then choose the furniture. But God reveals what furniture he wants first, and then how to put walls around it.

So we start with a piece of furniture in the inner room into which no man could go except the high priest once a year. That is all, and only then on one day. So this is God's own room. For this was built to be a dwelling place for God. This is where he was going to live on Earth and it is God's room and he only wanted one piece of furniture in it. It is a rather expensive and a rather elaborate piece of furniture.

Basically it is a chest—that is what the word "ark" means. It is a chest for keeping things in. That is one of the basic things you will have in your home – a chest of drawers or some kind of box. Even the simplest home that you visit today in other countries will have a box or chest in which the belongings are kept. Now here was God's chest of drawers if you like, his chest, his ark, made of very ordinary wood and yet covered with gold inside and out. You get this combination of the ordinary and the extraordinary right through this building – very ordinary wood covered with an extraordinary metal.

Many see in this combination the lovely combination of earthly and heavenly, the human and the divine, that we see ultimately in Jesus Christ himself. But here you have the ordinary become extraordinary for God. Now let us see what was kept inside this. There were three things, which speak to us very deeply. Indeed, there is a whole sermon of three points coming up.

There was first of all a pot of manna—that miraculous food sent down from heaven. Secondly, there were two lumps of stone – they can't have been very big – and engraved on that stone by God's own finger were the Ten Commandments. Also there was a branch of a tree with buds on it. It was a branch that once belonged to Moses' brother Aaron.

Now what do those three things mean? What do they say to you? I'll tell you what they say to me. They tell me that God meets my need at three different levels. He meets my need at the *material level*. "Give us this day our daily bread". If God didn't give us food we wouldn't have any. I thank God for providing my material needs and so do you: food, clothes, warmth.

The second need that I have is a *moral* one. I need someone to guide my conscience, to give me moral rules for life, to tell me how to live. God gave me my moral needs as well as my material – "For man does not live by bread alone but by every word that comes from the mouth of God."

The third need that I have, forgive the word—it lines up with the other two, is *mediatorial*. I need a mediator. For when I study the Ten Commandments I find I am not fit to come to God; I have broken them. So I need a priest who will on my behalf go to God for me, and the chosen priest in those days was Aaron. This is how God proved that Aaron was chosen. A lot of other people wanted to be priest in the tabernacle. There was quite a lot of rivalry and ambition. They all lined up and said they wanted to be priests. Why should Moses' brother have the monopoly? God said: let them each take a branch and let them present it to me; leave those branches before me, and the branch that has life in it, that buds, and blossoms, and produces fruit, that is my priest. The one that will bring forth fruit for me. When they studied the branches, one was budding, and it produced flowers and fruit. Aaron's rod that budded went in too.

God provides for your bodily needs, material needs, moral needs for your conscience to teach you how to live, and he provides you with a mediator when you fail and a priest who will go to him for you. It is no longer Aaron but the Lord Jesus. It is all kept in God's chest of drawers. Your three needs are perfectly met. That is the kind of God he is. He has enough in his store to meet every need you've got; and this is what that says to me.

There is a special lid made in one piece of solid gold, and it fits over this. No wood now, this is purely, heavenly, divine solid gold. These are not ordinary things covering that chest. The first is a solid slab of gold. I don't know what the weight must have been; it must have taken many people to carry a slab of gold called the seat. It is the only seat in the tabernacle. In one sense it is God's seat – his throne. But in another sense it is another kind of seat altogether. It is called the mercy seat. That pure slab of gold is a symbol of God's mercy, a place where sinful men can be met. Normally on that ledge you would have seen a dark brown caked mass of dried blood. Every year that high priest would bring some blood in and he would sprinkle it on there. The mercy of God can only come to you through blood. Only when Jesus shed his blood could God show mercy to your sins, and there it is.

Above the mercy seat were the cherubim. Now it doesn't just say angels, it says cherubim. There are two sorts of angels mentioned in the Bible: seraphim and cherubim. It seems as if God has chosen these two groups of angels for different functions. Seraphim are nearly always used to bring a message of mercy and love to people in forgiveness.

"Then flew one of the seraphim having taken off the altar a live coal and he touched my lips and said, 'Your iniquity is purged, taken away.'"

But the cherubim are God's messengers of justice and judgment. Cherubim guarded the way to the Garden of Eden after Adam and Eve were turned out. They stand for justice. Isn't that beautiful? The angels of judgment are looking down at the blood on the mercy seat. Does that say anything to you? If you are going to meet God, you dare not meet the cherubim, you dare not have the cherubim look into your life, you dare not have them looking at you. But if they are looking at the blood, then you are alright. This is saying to you that God's judging angels look at the blood of Jesus Christ and you can come to a mercy seat. That is God's furniture, all in one little piece of furniture, not very big, not as high as a pulpit, standing in a little room all by itself.

Having looked at the chest and the lid, now let us think about the decoration of this room. The ceiling as you look up, would have been decorated beautifully in that linen with the cherubim again – God's angels of judgment looking down on the scene below. The walls, gold leaf, and there (we shall come to it in a moment) a curtain hanging down. That is all. To me the most amazing thing about the decoration of that room is that with all the gorgeous gold and with the beautiful, embroidered ceiling and the gold furniture, there is a dirt floor – a sandy, soily floor, and no covering for the floor.

There was no room in our new centre like that! But here there was, and that beautiful piece of furniture stood on the bare soil. There is no instruction about carpets. Most religious buildings you will find in the Middle East to be sumptuously carpeted, but this was on the earth. God, when he dwells, has come right down to earth, he really has, as Jesus came right down into a dirty stable. This is God – he comes right down to the level of our ordinary life, down to the very soil from which we were made. Adam was made of the dust of the earth and God's tabernacle sits on the dust of the earth right where we are.

Now what about the lighting in there? You realise that with all this covering and no windows, there is no natural lighting in that room at all. Nor is there any artificial lighting – there is no candlestick. Yet that was the brightest part of this building. How? Because after it was finished and they said, "Now God, your room is ready. Come," he came. When God comes near, it is so bright that you and I could not stand the sight. Even when the high priest went in, he filled the place with incense smoke that took the glare off the glory of the Lord, the Shekinah glory. When God comes near it is brighter than the midday sun. When we get to heaven there will be neither natural nor artificial light needed – no sun, no moon, no lamps, for God will be in the midst of his people and he will be the light of that city. That was the brightest room in the house of God with no artificial lighting, no natural lighting and the glory of the Lord was in there. Can you imagine going in, even with the clouds of smoke and seeing this flashing piece of furniture, the walls glinting, and the light so bright that you might perhaps have to hold your cloak above your face – and God was there? One day you will see the glory of God like that and you won't be blinded; you will be given a new body by then, with eyes that can take it, and you will see the glory of the Lord.

There was a veil. That veil, that curtain said: Keep out, keep away. You notice that on it were cherubim looking in that direction; they are not looking at the mercy seat now. There are cherubim standing there, as they guarded the gate of Eden after Adam and Eve left. Here are cherubim, angels of judgment saying keep away; keep out, and the veil hung there for a millennium and a half keeping people away from God. Why? Because if you went in unauthorised and unprepared to that room you would be a dead man. The glory of the Lord would kill you.

We come now to the second room. Twice as large as the first, this room was literally called the Tent of Meeting; it was also called the Holy Place. We have spoken of the Holy of Holies where God alone dwelt, but here the priests of God met regularly. They came in regularly to meet with God. That is the place of God meeting with men. I am going to develop the theme that the three areas of the tabernacle tell us a great deal about the three persons of the godhead. One room tells us a lot about God the Father. That room where God and man meet tells us a lot about God the Son, about Christ. The court is full of meaning of the work of the Holy Spirit among people.

So let us look at the point where God meets men in the Holy Place. Here there is more furniture. Here there is artificial light because the glory of the Lord is further in and it is needed. We have here three items of furniture where God and man meet regularly. Therefore, I believe this is a picture of Christ because that is where God and man meet. The three items are the candlestick, which must have cost the equivalent of thousands of pounds, in solid gold. There are seven branches, three on one side three on the other and a large central one. It is a brilliant piece of lighting with seven lamps lighting up the gold-plated walls, glistening, showing the way, and people would come in here into light. One cannot help thinking of the one who said, "I am the light of the world" – if you follow me you won't walk in darkness; If you meet God in me, you'll walk in the light.

Right opposite was a little table: very small, human size, about the size of your kitchen table, with twelve loaves of bread on it. Jesus said, "I am the light of the world", "I am the bread of life", "Feed on me". The twelve loaves, signifying the twelve tribes, symbolises the unity of God's people feeding together on Christ and having everlasting life. The third piece of furniture is a very small altar. It was not used for sacrifices but for incense – a little pinch of incense burned on this and the cloud arose in front of the veil. Incense has always been a symbol of prayer and here is the prayer of Jesus symbolised first. Here is someone who for you is the light of the world, and the bread of life, and the one who ever lives to make intercession for you. When nobody else is praying for you, Jesus is. That is a lovely thought and he ever lives to do that and he is praying to God the Father for you.

Now we move out into the court itself, measuring seventy five by one hundred and fifty feet. I have been looking at God's approach to men, but now I am going to look at man's approach to God and we come in from the opposite direction. This speaks of the human side of the meeting between God and man. That is why the materials are much more ordinary – no gold in the outer court. There is a bit of bronze and some silver, but that is all. We are moving into ordinary realms now. This is the human part of the building. This symbolises the work of God the Holy Spirit in the human heart. Starting outside, imagine you are among the Israelites who are in tents. You would be looking at it from four sides. You would see the pure white curtain telling you that God is clean and holy and that if you are going to come inside, you must be too. As you look over the top you see the rather dull colour of the outside goatskin covering, looking very ordinary from the outside. There is not much to see from where you would be.

But notice that you have to get around to one end before you can get in. Whatever corner you come from, what direction you approach God from, sooner or later you have got to go through the same door. It is so obvious once you have said it. Now in our new Millmead Centre we had a door on every side. We tried to make it so convenient for everybody to get in from every angle; we just wanted people to come in. But God did not make it easy. There was one door and all had to come that way. Jesus said, "I am the door". It is only thieves who climb in other ways to try and get over the fence. If you want to come to God, you come through Jesus: "No-one comes to the Father but by me".

The curtain there is the same colour and embroidery as the curtain further in and the same as the colours of the ceiling in the room of God himself. It is as if Christ is reaching right out to you. The door into God's presence is a door of invitation. There are no angels of judgment frightening you away. The colours are there, but not the cherubim. The curtain seems to be saying: push the curtain aside; come in. It is an invitation door, and Jesus is also an invitation to you.

Do you remember *Pilgrim's Progress*? I do hope you have read it. Pilgrim wants to know how to reach the celestial city and an evangelist says, "Do you see yonder wicket gate?"

Pilgrim says, "Not quite."

"Well, do you see yonder shining light?"

"Yes."

"Well, make for that light and you'll come to a gate. Go through the gate."

Pilgrim sets off and he comes to the gate, and written above the gate is: "Whosoever will may come." He gets through the gate and he looks back and written above the gate is: "The elect according to the foreknowledge of God." That is a lovely picture in there of your choice and God's choice, and you will realise God's choice after you have made yours.

The next thing that you come to, as soon as you come through that door, as soon as you have started God's way, is a place where life is taken, where blood is shed, where sacrifice is made. You can get no nearer to God until you have been there. That is why, very shortly after Bunyan's pilgrim goes through the gate that leads him towards God, he comes to a hill, somewhat rising, and on the top stands a cross. He climbs towards it and, as he looks at the cross, the burden on his shoulders looses from off his back, tumbles down the hill, and it is gone.

I want you to notice that the first thing you need to do if you are going to meet with God is to get to the place of sacrifice: the place where blood has been shed, the place where an offering has been made for sin. You cannot get any nearer to God until you have been to the cross. So once you have realised, and repented, and turned into God's way, it is the altar that you go to.

Now we did not put an altar in our new building and we never use the word – we do not need it. The altar we have is a hill outside a city wall that had a cross on it. There were horns on that altar to tie the animals to. They are sharp, spiked horns. Let them speak to you of the nails that tied the Lamb of God to the place of death and sacrifice. Let those four horns say to you: come from the four winds and from the four corners of the earth, but come to this place. "I, if I be lifted up, will draw all men to me."

We move on past the altar and the first thing we come to after the altar is a place to wash. I want you to notice the order: come to the cross and then get clean. It is not, "Get clean first and then come" – that washbasin is not outside the door. There is an order to get right with God and the first thing is to get the guilt of your past sin dealt with and then to get the power of your future sin taken away. The first thing is to get peace with God, then to get clean before God. It must be this way around. It is extraordinary how many people think that God's way of salvation is, "put yourself right first and then come". No, God has provided a place to get you right. Then he will get you clean as you come nearer and deeper into fellowship with him.

They may have washed in the top or the bottom of the

basin (or washed their hands in the top and their feet in the bottom I don't know; we are not given the details), but one thing is very interesting. It was made out of the ladies' vanity mirrors. I don't know what that says to you, but it says something to the men too. In those days they did not use glass mirrors, they did not have glass and quicksilver, so they could not make a mirror such as we have. They would take a piece of bronze and they would polish and polish it. It was not as good as the mirrors we have but it was pretty good. They would use this to get their hair straight and to make themselves presentable and that is what we use mirrors for. Moses asked them to bring their mirrors to make a place of washing. It is almost as if God was saying that the thing that he needed to get people clean of is their pride, their vanity and self-centredness – looking at yourself and thinking about yourself. God had to get that washed away and then they could come into closer fellowship.

I want to ask this: how far in can people come? We have seen that God has come down to dwell with people and he is reaching out. The colour of the curtains says that. The Holy Spirit is necessary to start you off; the Holy Spirit will bring you to the door; the Holy Spirit will convict you of sin, righteousness and judgment and get you to the cross; the Holy Spirit will do the sanctifying. That outer court is the Holy Spirit's work, but how far in can we go? For the Israelite, we have gone as far in as he was allowed to go.

Only the priest could push open the second curtain, and only the High Priest could push open the third. So the ordinary people stayed out there. But not the Christian. How far can the Christian go? Much further—let me take you now right in because you are a Christian and in Christ you can come in Christ, you can come right in. So let us go in. We are told in the New Testament that believers in Christ are a priesthood. That is why we never use the word "priest".

Every living member of the Body of Christ now is in the priesthood. That is one reason I don't dress differently from any Christian – because I am not any different.

We are priests unto God and therefore we can go straight through that second curtain. Israelites could not do so – except a few of them who were priests could go through – but we can come right in. When we come through, we enter into Christ's ministry, we share it. Jesus said, "I am the light of the world," but then he also said to his disciples, "You are the light of the world." It was one of the few titles he gave to both himself and them. "Let your light shine before men." Don't put it under a bushel but put it on a lamp stand. Let them see it.

You can share in this ministry of illuminating a dark world and the table becomes for us a wonderful symbol of our fellowship in Christ, sharing the bread together. The table is something that we put in our new building – a table where we sit down together and have a meal together in Christ. In the tabernacle there was a table of the shewbread, something that the priests ate together.

The ministry of intercession becomes ours too. We can now join in the work of the altar. We could never join in the work of that tabernacle altar, but we can join with the one who ever lives to make intercession for us, and we too can pray for someone else in need. We can join our prayers to those of Christ and they can ascend to God the Father. Can we go any further than this? Yes, we can. Can we push aside that third veil? Let me tell you now something wonderful: it is not there. It has gone and there is only one room now. There was a day when Jesus hung on a cross, nailed to that cross, and they rent his body. As they rent his body, the veil of the temple was rent in two, from the top to the bottom. No man did that; it was God's hands that did that. God ripped up that veil and said, "It's finished." All that has gone. The way is wide open now. You can come right in. Jesus has died.

So Jesus went through the veil, which was his flesh. Do you understand that deep symbolism? The veil hung there to hide the glory of God; and the flesh of Jesus, which had the fullness of the godhead bodily dwelling within, the flesh of Jesus veiled the godhead. Only once in his lifetime did the glory break through that veil and they saw Jesus transfigured on the mountain. But when that veil of his body was rent on the cross, God tore up that veil. It is not there and those who come in through Christ and have been to the cross and are washed by the sanctification of the Holy Spirit, and have become the light of the world, are breaking bread together, and offering intercession to God – can look straight ahead and go straight ahead into the Holy of Holies. Here is the New Testament basis for that, in Hebrews 10:19–25, ESV.

Therefore, brothers, since we have confidence to enter the holy places by the blood of Jesus, by the new and living way that he opened for us through the curtain, that is, through his flesh, and since we have a great priest over the house of God, let us draw near with a true heart in full assurance of faith, with our hearts sprinkled clean from an evil conscience and our bodies washed with pure water. Let us hold fast the confession of our hope without wavering, for he who promised is faithful. And let us consider how to stir up one another to love and good works, not neglecting to meet together, as is the habit of some, but encouraging one another, and all the more as you see the Day drawing near.

As the letter to the Hebrews speaks of coming right in, it begins to speak of our relationship to each other – not just coming into God but coming in to be close to each other.

Now we come to the boards of the tabernacle. The truth is

that in Jesus Christ you can not only come right in to every part of the building, you actually become part of the building itself and house God within your own body.

Each board was fifteen or seventeen feet (depending on what the cubit was), about two and a quarter/two and a half feet wide, straight upright boards, all of equal height, with two tenons – two feet at the bottom. They were sunk into heavy silver blocks with a slot in, two blocks for each board. But if that was all it had, they would have collapsed in the first wind at that height in sand. How did they stay up? They held each other up and they were linked with bars, slotted through with hooks so that they were a strong structure and helped each other up, standing in the desert. Every one of those boards speaks to me of a believer linked with other believers and together forming the house of God on earth.

Let us dwell on that a moment. The acacia is a funny tree. It grows in the Sinai desert, but it grows crooked. It is terrible wood, full of knots, all bent in the grain. Those very ordinary, crooked, earthy trees God could make into his house. Do you know what had to be done? They had to be chopped down and cut off from the earth. Then they had to be cut and shaped themselves, and then they were overlaid with gold, and they stood upright and straight. The wood used to be crooked and earthy, but now it is gold, it is upright, and it is straight. Do you see the meaning? Do you realise that now they are not only standing straight, they are separated from the earth in which they once had their life by the silver, which is the symbol of redemption. Between the believer and the world to which he used to belong is the redemption not of silver or gold but of the precious blood of Jesus. Standing upright with both feet in Christ – not one but both, a little touch that makes the board so human. Both feet standing in Christ and linked together, they stand upright, equal in height before God, no one board standing out among the others – linked together, covered with Christ. Because they are gold-plated they can now reflect the glory of God. This very ordinary crooked wood is now showing the glory of God.

We who believe are carefully joined together in Christ as parts of a beautiful, constantly growing temple of God, and you also are joined with him and with each other by the Spirit, and are part of this dwelling place of God. Do you understand now why a church building is made for people and the people are made for God? The tabernacle was a structure for God to live in and it had to be just as it was, but we no longer believe that God inhabits buildings made with hands. The temple of the living God is made up of believers, so we design buildings that are just right for believers to meet in. When the believers are meeting in a building, then God himself is dwelling there in his holy temple.

ABOUT DAVID PAWSON

A speaker and author with uncompromising faithfulness to the Holy Scriptures, David brings clarity and a message of urgency to Christians to uncover hidden treasures in God's Word.

Born in England in 1930, David began his career with a degree in Agriculture from Durham University. When God intervened and called him to become a Minister, he completed an MA in Theology at Cambridge University and served as a Chaplain in the Royal Air Force for three years. He moved on to pastor several churches, including the Millmead Centre in Guildford, which became a model for many UK church leaders. In 1979, the Lord led him into an international ministry. His current itinerant ministry is predominantly to church leaders. David and his wife Enid currently reside in the county of Hampshire in the UK.

Over the years, he has written a large number of books, booklets, and daily reading notes. His extensive and very accessible overviews of the books of the Bible have been published and recorded in *Unlocking the Bible*. Millions of copies of his teachings have been distributed in more than 120 countries, providing a solid biblical foundation.

He is reputed to be the "most influential Western preacher in China" through the broadcast of his best-selling *Unlocking the Bible* series into every Chinese province by Good TV. In the UK, David's teachings are often broadcast on Revelation TV.

Countless believers worldwide have also benefited from his generous decision in 2011 to make available his extensive audio video teaching library free of charge at **www.davidpawson.org** and we have recently uploaded all of David's video to a dedicated channel on **www.youtube.com**

TAKE A LOOK AT YOUTUBE
www.youtube.com/user/DavidPawsonMinistry

THE EXPLAINING SERIES
BIBLICAL TRUTH SIMPLY EXPLAINED

If you have been blessed reading this book, we have more books available in David's Explaining Series. Please register to download for free by visiting **www.explainingbiblicaltruth.global**

Other booklets in the *Explaining* series include:
The Amazing Story of Jesus
The Resurrection: *The Heart of Christianity*
Studying the Bible
Being Anointed and Filled with the Holy Spirit
New Testament Baptism
How to study a book of the Bible: Jude
The Key Steps to Becoming a Christian
What the Bible says about Money
What the Bible says about Work
Grace – *Undeserved Favour, Irresistible Force or Unconditional Forgiveness?*
Eternally secure? – *What the Bible says about being saved*
De-Greecing the Church – The impact of Greek thinking on Christian beliefs
Three texts often taken out of context: *Expounding the truth and exposing error*
The Trinity
The Truth about Christmas

They will also be available to purchase as print copies from:
Amazon or **www.thebookdepository.com**

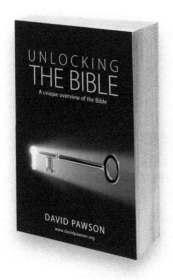

UNLOCKING
THE BIBLE

A unique overview of both the Old and New Testaments, from internationally acclaimed evangelical speaker and author David Pawson. *Unlocking the Bible* opens up the Word of God in a fresh and powerful way. Avoiding the small detail of verse by verse studies, it sets out the epic story of God and his people in Israel. The culture, historical background and people are introduced and the teaching applied to the modern world. Eight volumes have been brought into one compact and easy to use guide to cover both the Old and New Testaments in one massive omnibus edition. *The Old Testament: The Maker's Instructions* (The five books of law); *A Land and A Kingdom* (Joshua, Judges, Ruth, 1&2 Samuel, 1&2 Kings); *Poems of Worship and Wisdom* (Psalms, Song of Solomon, Proverbs, Ecclesiastes, Job); *Decline and Fall of an Empire* (Isaiah, Jeremiah and other prophets); *The Struggle to Survive* (Chronicles and prophets of exile); *The New Testament: The Hinge of History* (Mathew, Mark, Luke, John and Acts); *The Thirteenth Apostle* (Paul and his letters); *Through Suffering to Glory* (Hebrews, the letters of James, Peter and Jude, the Book of Revelation). Already an international bestseller.

OTHER LANGUAGES

Unlocking the Bible is available in book, video and audio formats and has been translated into other languages.

WATCH DAVID'S INTRO
www.davidpawson.com/utbintro

WATCH
www.davidpawson.com/utbwatch

LISTEN
www.davidpawson.com/utblisten

PURCHASE THE BOOK
www.davidpawson.com/utbbuybook

PURCHASE THE EBOOK
www.davidpawson.com/utbbuykindle

PURCHASE THE DVD
www.davidpawson.com/utbbuydvd

PURCHASE USB
FLASH DRIVE INCLUDING:
- ALL VIDEO (MP4)
- ALL AUDIO TRACKS (MP3)
- CHARTS (PDF)

www.davidpawson.com/buyusb

OTHER TEACHINGS
BY DAVID PAWSON

For the most up to date list of David's Books
go to: **www.davidpawsonbooks.com**

To purchase David's Teachings
go to: **www.davidpawson.com**